Fun-Schooling Science Handbook

ALL ABOUT SPACE

Explore the Universe!

Research, Create, Play, Experiment & Learn

The Thinking Tree

ALL ABOUT SPACE

Explore the Universe!
Research, Create, Play, Experiment & Learn
Cover 18 Essential Educational Subjects While Learning about Space!
FUN For ALL Ages!

STEP-BY-STEP SCIENCE ACTIVITIES YOU CAN TRY AT HOME

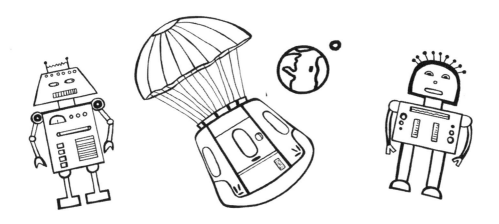

Created By:
Sarah Janisse Brown, Melissa Knorr
Alexandra Bretush & Notika Pachinko

FUNSCHOOLINGBOOKS.COM

ALL ABOUT
SPACE

NaMe: & Age:

Date:

AddreSS:

PHoNe NuMber:

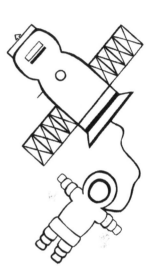

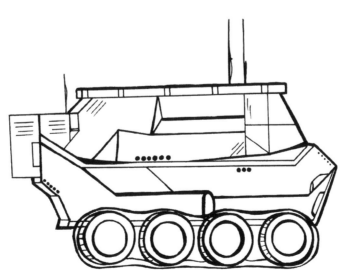

This Curriculum Covers:

- Space & Science
- The Planets
- The Solar System
- Space Exploration
- Space Discoveries
- Reading Activities
- Handwriting Practice
- Creative Writing
- Spelling Games
- Mathematics
- Research Projects
- Space Exploration History
- Art & Drawing
- Library Skills
- Unit Studies
- Logic Games
- Experiments
- Crafts

INSTRUCTIONS
LEARN ALL ABOUT SPACE!

Draw or Write about FIVE THINGS
That you want to know about Space!

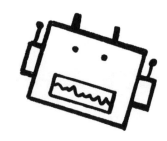

ACTION STEPS:

1. Go to the library or bookstore.
2. Bring home a stack of at least FIVE interesting books about space.
3. Choose some that have diagrams, instructions and illustrations.

SCHOOL SUPPLIES NEEDED:

Pencils, Colored Pencils
& Gel Pens.

Each Craft Project or Experiment
Will have a Supply List!

CARDBOARD x2

Dixie cup

Tape

INDEX CARDS

Marshmallows x2

Mini Marshmallows

STRAWS

Rubber bands

GO TO THE LIBRARY AND CHOOSE SIX BOOKS ABOUT SPACE TO USE AS SCHOOL BOOKS!

1. Write down the titles on each book cover below.

2. Keep your stack of books in a safe place so you can read a few pages from your books daily.

3. Ask your teacher how many pages to do each day in this Journal. Five to ten pages is normal for kids your age.

4. If you get more books use the next page!

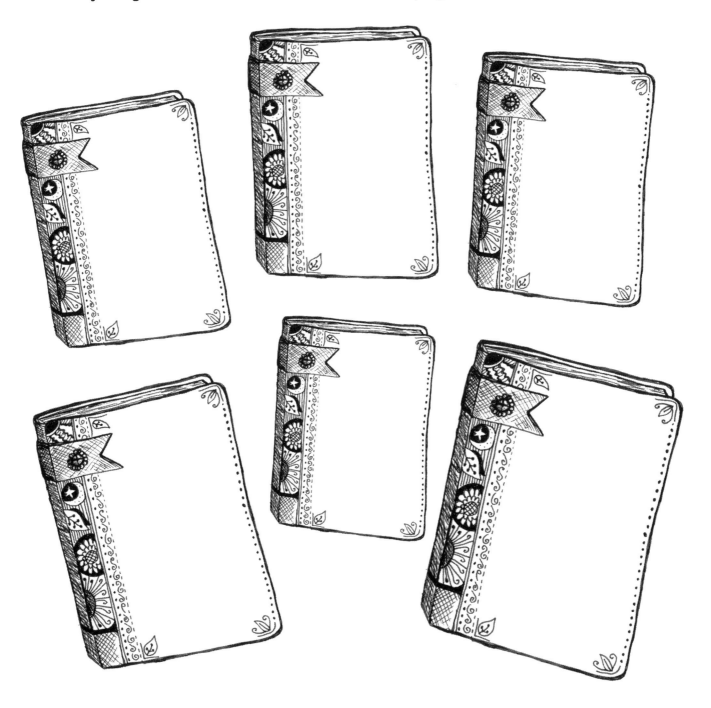

MY LEARNING LIST

Additional Books & Documentaries

TITLE: DATE:

_____
_____
_____
_____
_____
_____
_____
_____
_____
_____
_____
_____
_____
_____
_____
_____
_____
_____
_____
_____
_____
_____
_____
_____
_____
_____
_____
_____
_____
_____
_____
_____

LET'S HAVE SOME FUN!

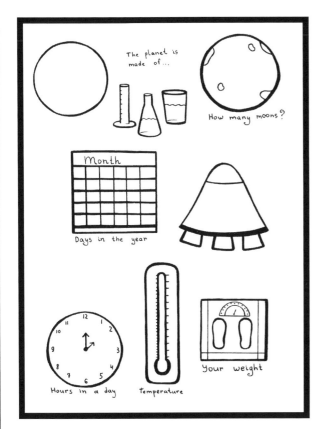

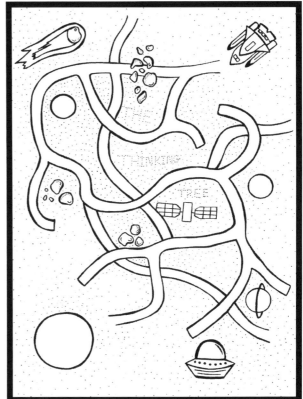

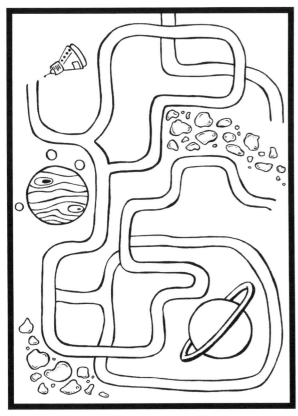

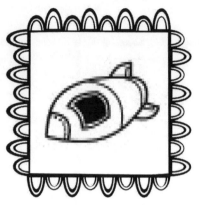

Spend Time reading your books!

Write and draw about What your Learned!

READING TIME

Today's Date:

_____

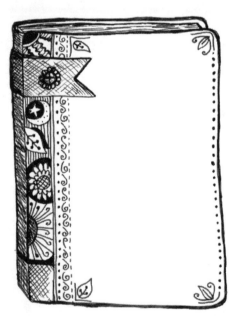

SET YOUR TIMER FOR 30 MINUTES!
READ UNTIL THE TIMER STOPS!

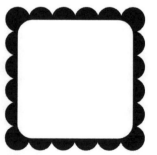

Date:

READING TIME

Copy an interesting paragraph
or list from your book.
Book Title:_____ **Page #**_____

_____
_____
_____
_____
_____
_____
_____
_____
_____
_____
_____
_____
_____
_____
_____

Illustration

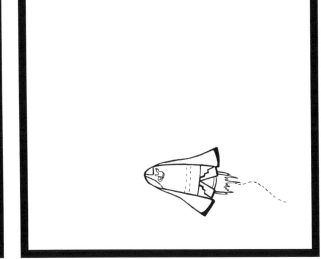

WHAT IS A GALAXY?

_____
_____
_____
_____
_____
_____
_____
_____
_____
_____
_____
_____

SCIENCE PROJECT:
Galaxy in a jar

Jar

Cotton Balls

Glitter   Water

Materials:
Jar, 2-3 tempera paints, cotton balls, water

Instructions:

1. Fill 1/3 of the jar with water.

2. Add several drops of paint to the water, put the lid on, and shake to mix the paint and water.

3. Add a bit of glitter.

4. Stretch cotton balls and add them to the water until the bottom is filled with cotton, pressing them down into the water with a stick or butter knife.
Fill another 1/3 of the jar with water, add several drops of contrasting paint, and repeat steps 2-4.
Fill the final 1/3 of the jar with water and repeat steps 2-4.

SPACE DISCOVERIES

CHOOSE A PERSON OR A TOPIC TO STUDY

(Astronauts, NASA Engineers, Astronomers, etc.)

Name: _____

_____

_____

_____

_____

_____

_____

_____

_____

_____

_____

_____

Draw a diagram or illustration:

VOCABULARY BUILDING

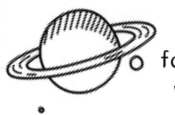

Look in your Space Books
for **FOUR** words with more than **TEN** letters.
Write the words and their definitions below:

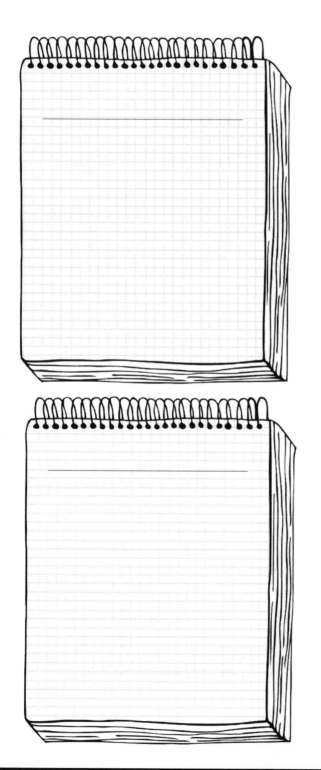

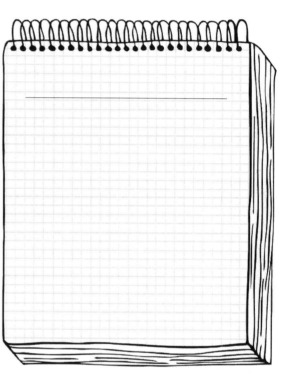

Spelling Time

Find 20 Words with 8 letters each.

Look in your books for words.

Write the words here:

_____   _____

_____   _____

_____   _____

_____   _____

_____   _____

_____   _____

_____   _____

_____   _____

_____   _____

_____   _____

COLOR AND FINISH THIS PICTURE

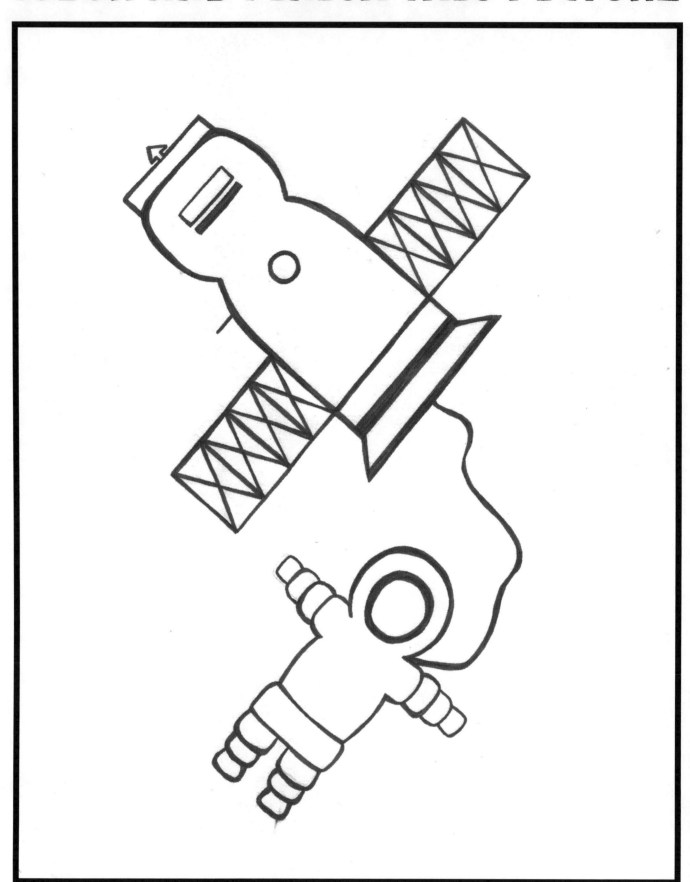

The Sun

What is the Sun made of?

_____
_____
_____
_____

What is the temperature on the Sun?

_____

Write down **3** interesting facts about the Sun:

1._____
_____

2._____
_____

3._____
_____

DRAW YOUR OWN SUN

COLOR THIS PAGE

DESIGN YOUR OWN
SPACESHIP

The Moon

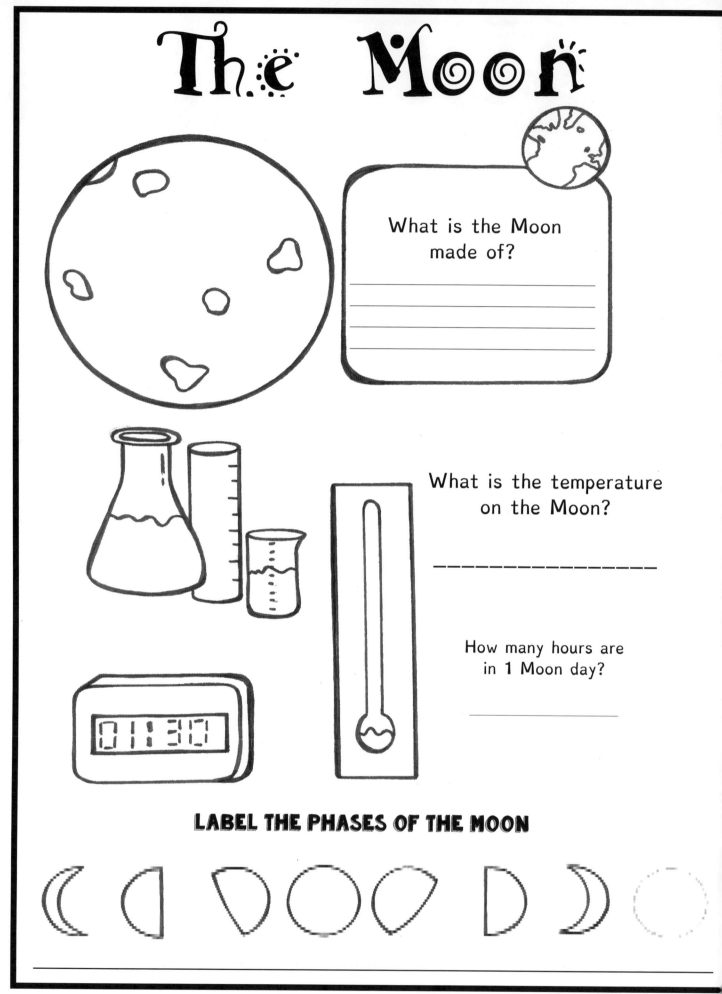

What is the Moon made of?

What is the temperature on the Moon?

How many hours are in 1 Moon day?

LABEL THE PHASES OF THE MOON

Write down **3** interesting facts about the Moon:

1._____

_____

2._____

_____

3._____

_____

DRAW YOUR OWN MOON

SPACE DISCOVERIES
CHOOSE A PERSON OR A TOPIC TO STUDY
(Astronauts, NASA Engineers, Astronomers, etc.)

Name:_____

_____
_____
_____
_____
_____
_____
_____
_____
_____
_____
_____
_____
_____

Draw a diagram or illustration:

NEWS FROM SPACE

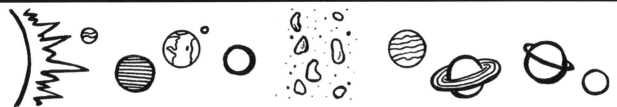

WHAT WOULD YOU LIKE TO LEARN ABOUT SPACE?

_____

_____

_____

_____

_____

_____

_____

_____

DRAW THE CURRENT PHASE OF THE MOON

SPACE IN THE NEWS

FIND PAST OR CURRENT NEWS ARTICLES AND STORIES,
AND WRITE OR DRAW ABOUT THEM IN THIS SECTION

SCIENCE PROJECT:
Making Craters on the Moon
WHY DOES THE MOON HAVE CRATERS?

Materials:
4 cups of flour, ½ cup baby oil, small pebbles, and a round cake pan

Pebbles

Round
Cake Pan

Instructions:

Mix the flour and oil together.
Put mixture in the cake pan.
Drop pebbles in the mixture.

Write down the results

_____
_____
_____
_____
_____
_____
_____

CREATIVE WRITING

Names & Descriptions of Characters:

_____

_____

_____

_____

Title:

_____

_____

_____

_____

_____

_____

_____

_____

_____

_____

_____

_____

_____

_____

_____

_____

_____

COLOR AND FINISH THIS PICTURE

SELECT A SPACE MISSION TO LEARN MORE ABOUT

The name of the mission:

_____

Write about this mission.
When and where did it take place? Who was involved?
How did it end?

_____

_____

_____

_____

_____

_____

_____

_____

_____

_____

_____

_____

_____

_____

LEARN ABOUT PHASES OF THE MOON

Label the phases of the moon

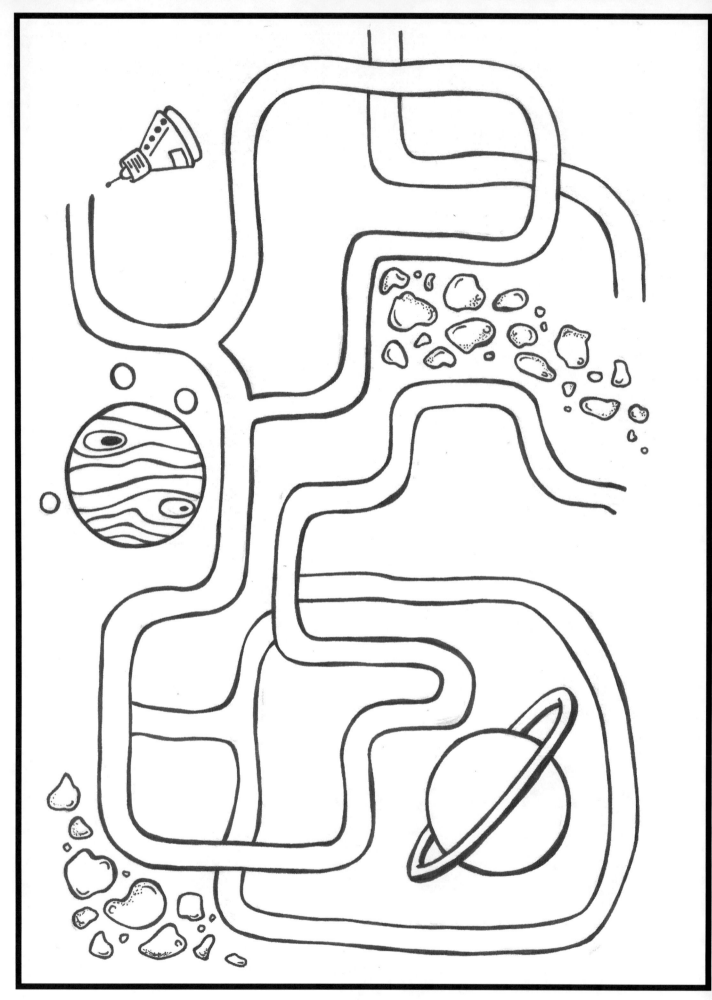

MY SPACE DRAWINGS AND NOTES

SPACE DISCOVERIES

CHOOSE A PERSON OR A TOPIC TO STUDY

(Astronauts, NASA Engineers, Astronomers, etc.)

Name:_____

_____

_____

_____

_____

_____

_____

_____

_____

_____

_____

_____

_____

_____

Draw a diagram or illustration:

LEARN ABOUT AN ECLIPSE

_____
_____
_____
_____
_____
_____
_____
_____
_____
_____
_____

LEARN ABOUT
THE ASTEROID BELT

LEARN ABOUT
SATELLITES IN SPACE

Why are there satellites in space?

_____
_____
_____
_____
_____
_____
_____
_____

Spelling Time

Find 20 Words with **7** letters each.
Look in your books for words.
Write the words here:

_____	_____
_____	_____
_____	_____
_____	_____
_____	_____
_____	_____
_____	_____
_____	_____
_____	_____
_____	_____

SCIENCE PROJECT:
Moon Rock

Materials:
2 cups of flour, 1 cup of salt, water, black paint, and lots of glitter

Instructions:

1. Combine the ingredients.
2. Mold your rock and add lumps and dents.
3. Let dry.

WRITE DOWN AND DRAW THE RESULT

CREATIVE WRITING

Names & Descriptions of Characters:

_____

_____

_____

_____

Title:

_____

_____

_____

_____

_____

_____

_____

_____

_____

_____

_____

_____

_____

_____

_____

_____

Mercury

What is Mercury made of?

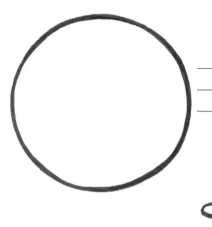

_____

_____

_____

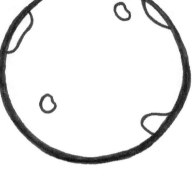

How many moons does Mercury have?

_____

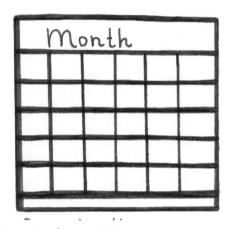

How many days are in 1 Mercury year?

_____

What is the temperature on Mercury?

How much would you weigh if you were on Mercury?

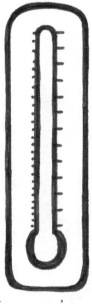

_____

Write down **3** interesting facts about Mercury:

1._____

_____

2._____

_____

3._____

_____

DRAW YOUR OWN MERCURY

MY SPACE DRAWINGS AND NOTES

READING TIME

Copy an interesting paragraph
or list from your book.
Book Title:_____ **Page #**_____

_____
_____
_____
_____
_____
_____
_____
_____
_____
_____
_____
_____
_____
_____

Date:

Illustration

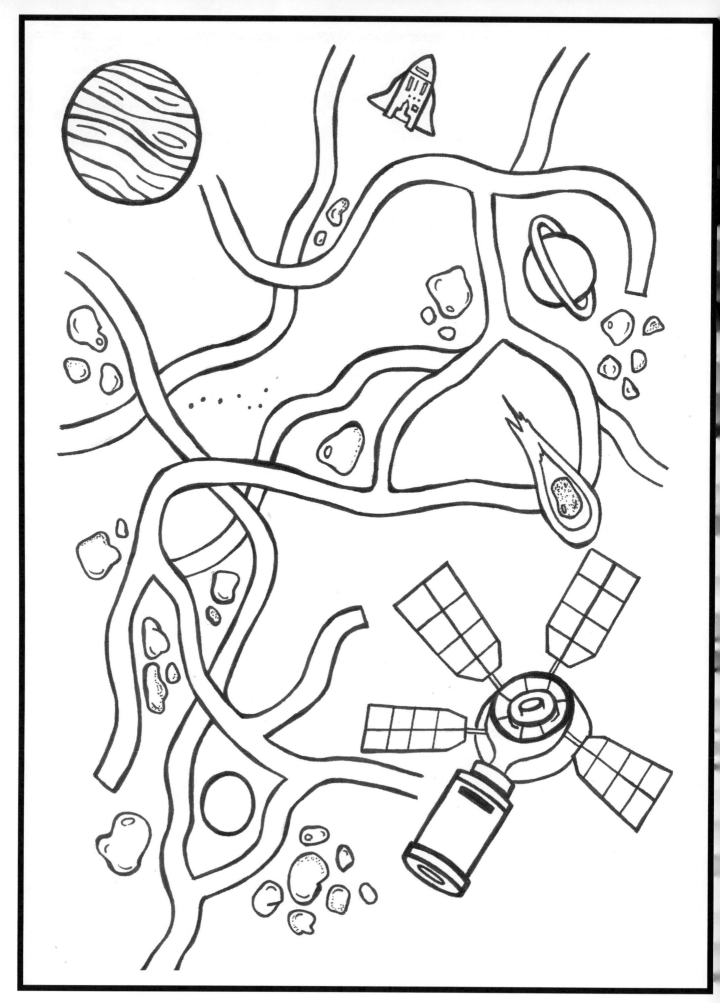

NEWS FROM SPACE

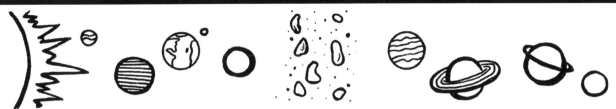

WHAT WOULD YOU LIKE TO LEARN ABOUT SPACE?

_____

_____

_____

_____

_____

_____

_____

DRAW THE CURRENT PHASE OF THE MOON

SPACE IN THE NEWS
FIND PAST OR CURRENT NEWS ARTICLES AND STORIES, AND WRITE OR DRAW ABOUT THEM IN THIS SECTION

Venus

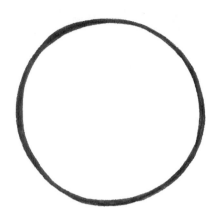

How many hours are in 1 Venus day?

How many moons does Venus have?

How many days are in 1 Venus year?

What is Venus made of?

What is the temperature on Venus?

How much would you weigh if you were on Venus?

Write down **3** interesting facts about Venus:

1._____

_____

2._____

_____

3._____

_____

DRAW YOUR OWN VENUS

CREATIVE WRITING

Names & Descriptions of Characters:

_____

_____

_____

_____

_____

Title:

_____

_____

_____

_____

_____

_____

_____

_____

_____

_____

_____

_____

_____

_____

_____

MY SPACE DRAWINGS AND NOTES

SELECT A SPACE MISSION TO LEARN MORE ABOUT

The name of the mission:

_____

DATE:

_____

Write about this mission.
When and where did it take place? Who was involved?
How did it end?

_____
_____
_____
_____
_____
_____
_____
_____
_____
_____
_____
_____
_____

VOCABULARY BUILDING

Look in your Space Books
for **FOUR** words with more than **TEN** letters.
Write the words and their definitions below:

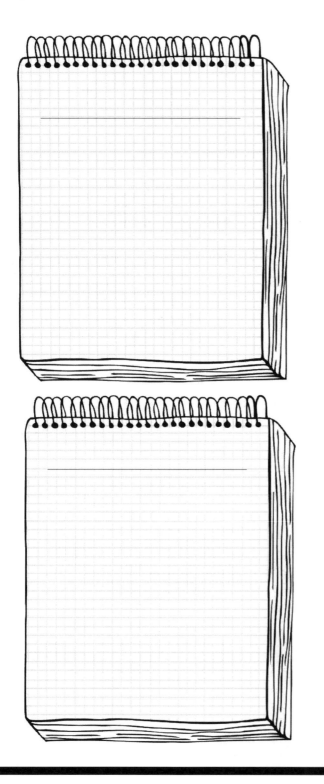

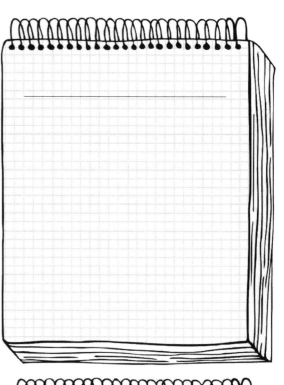

Spelling Time

Find 20 Words with 6 letters each.

Look in your books for words.

Write the words here:

_____   _____

_____   _____

_____   _____

_____   _____

_____   _____

_____   _____

_____   _____

_____   _____

_____   _____

CREATIVE WRITING

Names & Descriptions of Characters:

_____

_____

_____

_____

Title:

_____

_____

_____

_____

_____

_____

_____

_____

_____

_____

_____

_____

_____

_____

_____

_____

Earth

What is Earth
made of?

_____

_____

_____

_____

_____

_____

How many hours are
in **1 Earth** day?

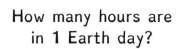

How many moons does
Earth have?

_____

How many days are
in **1 Earth** year?

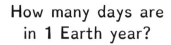

What is the average
temperature on Earth?

_____

Write down **3** interesting facts about Earth:

1. _____

2. _____

3. _____

DRAW YOUR OWN EARTH

SPACE DISCOVERIES

CHOOSE A PERSON OR A TOPIC TO STUDY

(Astronauts, NASA Engineers, Astronomers, etc.)

Date:

Name:_____

_____

_____

_____

_____

_____

_____

_____

_____

_____

_____

_____

_____

_____

Draw a diagram or illustration:

DESIGN YOUR OWN LAUNCH PAD

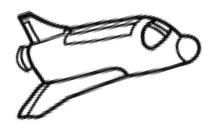

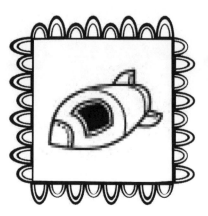

Today's Date:

_____

READING TIME

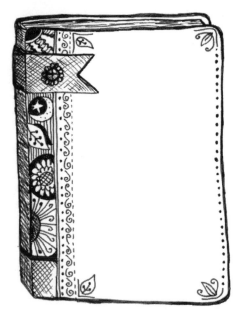

SET YOUR TIMER FOR 30
MINUTES!
READ UNTIL THE TIMER STOPS!

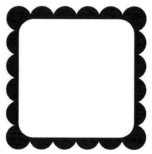

Date:

READING TIME

Copy an interesting paragraph
or list from your book.

Book Title:_____ **Page #**_____

_____

_____

_____

_____

_____

_____

_____

_____

_____

_____

_____

_____

_____

Illustration

WATCH A DOCUMENTARY ABOUT SPACE

Notes:

Ideas:

Rating:
AWFUL
BAD
LAME
YUCKY
OKAY
NICE
GOOD
GREAT
SUPER
AMAZING

Title:

Topic:

Use this space to doodle

INTERESTING FACTS ABOUT THIS DOCUMENTARY:

_____
_____
_____
_____
_____

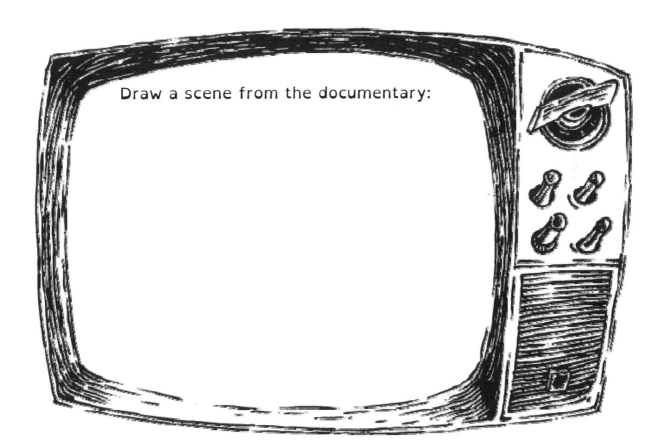

Draw a scene from the documentary:

Write a review:

_____
_____
_____
_____
_____

INTERESTING FACTS ABOUT THIS DOCUMENTARY:

Mars

What is Mars made of?

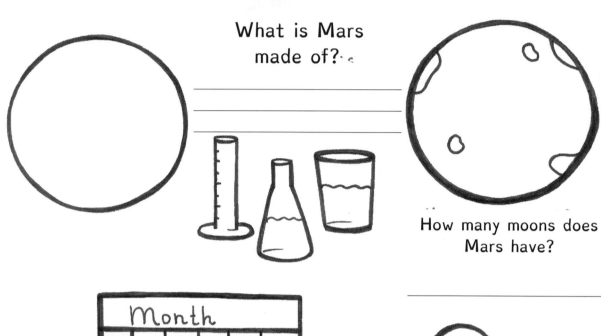

_____

_____

_____

How many moons does Mars have?

_____

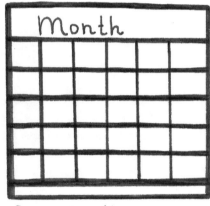

How many days are in 1 Mars year?

_____

What is the temperature on Mars?

_____

How much would you weigh if you were on Mars?

_____

Write down **3** interesting facts about Mars:

1._____

_____

2._____

_____

3._____

_____

DRAW YOUR OWN MARS

MY SPACE DRAWINGS AND NOTES

NEWS FROM SPACE

WHAT WOULD YOU LIKE TO LEARN ABOUT SPACE?

_____
_____
_____
_____
_____
_____
_____
_____

DRAW THE CURRENT PHASE OF THE MOON

SPACE IN THE NEWS
FIND PAST OR CURRENT NEWS ARTICLES AND STORIES, AND WRITE OR DRAW ABOUT THEM IN THIS SECTION

CREATE YOUR OWN ROBOT

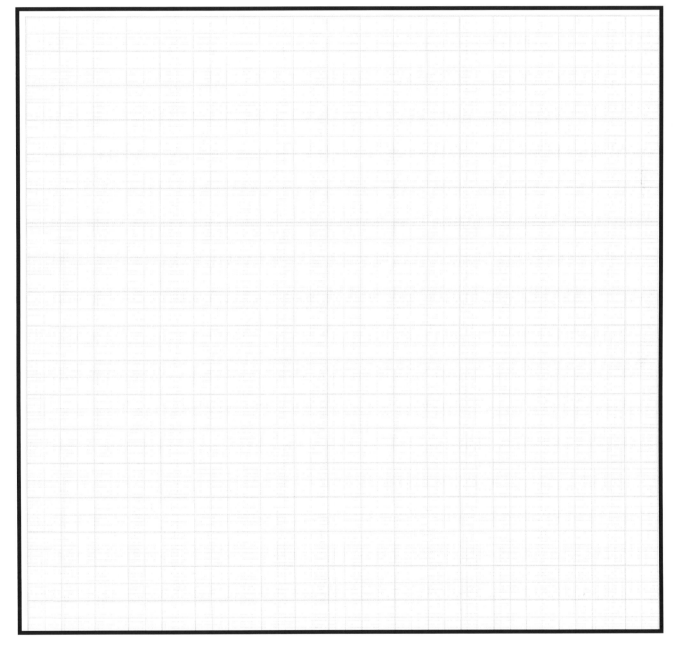

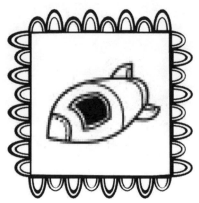

Spend Time reading your books!

Write and draw about what you learned!

READING TIME

Today's Date:

_____

SET YOUR TIMER FOR 30 MINUTES!
READ UNTIL THE TIMER STOPS!

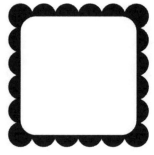

Date:

READING TIME

Copy an interesting paragraph
or list from your book.

Book Title:_____ **Page #**_____

_____
_____
_____
_____
_____
_____
_____
_____
_____
_____
_____
_____
_____
_____

Illustration

VOCABULARY BUILDING

Look in your Space Books
for **FOUR** words with more than **TEN** letters.
Write the words and their definitions below:

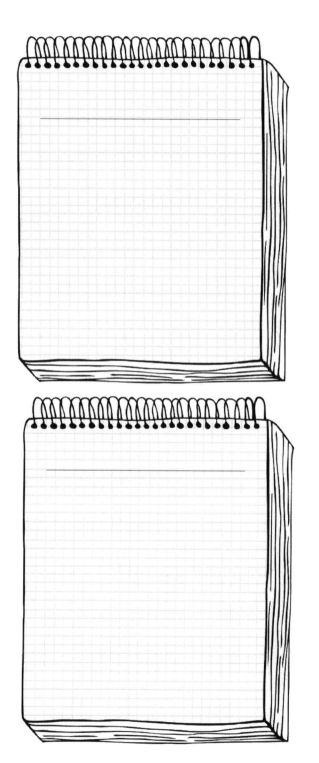

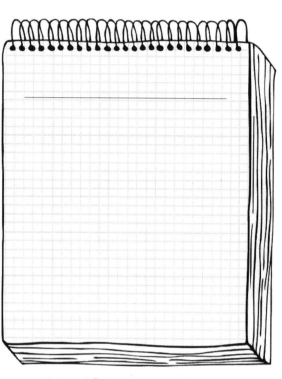

Spelling Time

Find 20 Words with 5 letters each.

Look in your books for words.

Write the words here:

_____   _____

_____   _____

_____   _____

_____   _____

_____   _____

_____   _____

_____   _____

_____   _____

_____   _____

_____   _____

Jupiter

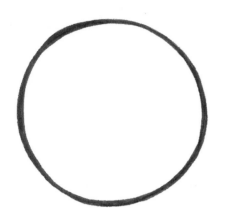

How many moons does
Jupiter have?

How many hours are
in 1 Jupiter day?

How many days
are in 1 Jupiter
year?

What is Jupiter
made of?

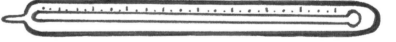

What is the temperature on Jupiter?

How much would you weigh if you were
on Jupiter?

Write down **3** interesting facts about Jupiter:

1._____

_____

2._____

_____

3._____

_____

DRAW YOUR OWN JUPITER

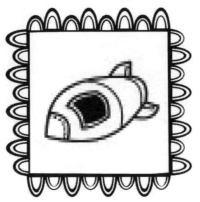

READING TIME

Today's Date:

_____

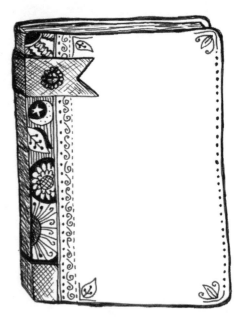

SET YOUR TIMER FOR 30
MINUTES!
READ UNTIL THE TIMER STOPS!

SELECT A SPACE MISSION TO LEARN MORE ABOUT

The name of the mission:

_____

DATE:

_____

Write about this mission.
When and where did it take place? Who was involved?
How did it end?

_____

_____

_____

_____

_____

_____

_____

_____

_____

_____

_____

_____

_____

_____

COLOR AND FINISH THIS PICTURE

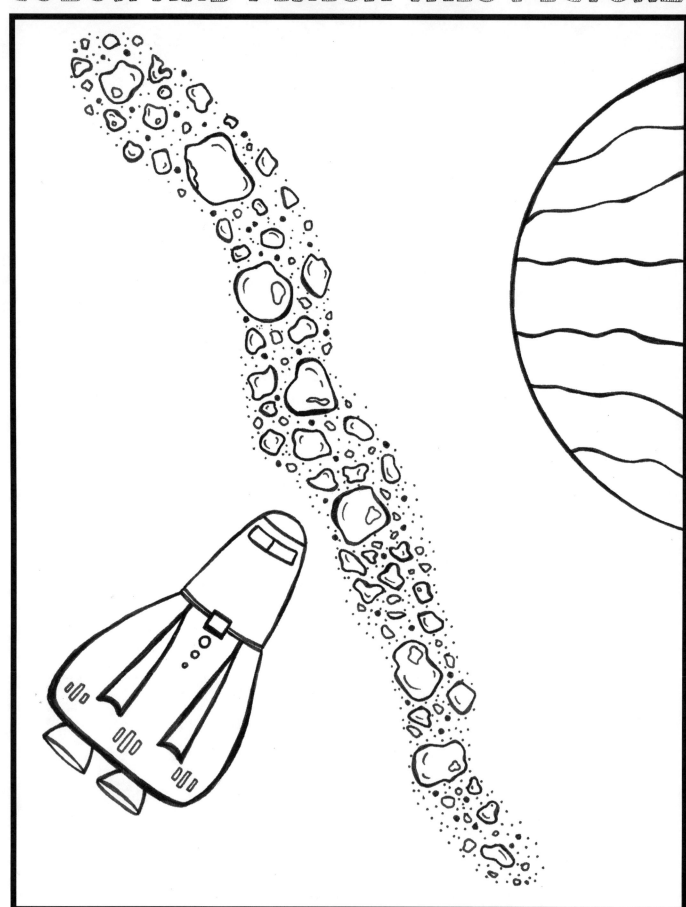

SPACE DISCOVERIES

CHOOSE A PERSON OR A TOPIC TO STUDY

(Astronauts, NASA Engineers, Astronomers, etc.)

Name:_____

_____

_____

_____

_____

_____

_____

_____

_____

_____

_____

_____

_____

_____

Draw a diagram or illustration:

Saturn

What is Saturn made of?

_____
_____
_____

How many moons does Saturn have?

_____

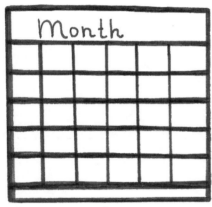

How many days are in **1** Saturn year?

What is the temperature on Saturn?

_____

How much would you weigh if you were on Saturn?

_____

Write down **3** interesting facts about Saturn:

1.＿＿＿＿＿＿＿＿＿＿＿＿＿＿＿＿＿＿＿＿＿＿＿＿＿＿＿＿＿

2.＿＿＿＿＿＿＿＿＿＿＿＿＿＿＿＿＿＿＿＿＿＿＿＿＿＿＿＿＿

3.＿＿＿＿＿＿＿＿＿＿＿＿＿＿＿＿＿＿＿＿＿＿＿＿＿＿＿＿＿

DRAW YOUR OWN SATURN

DESIGN YOUR OWN ROBOT

  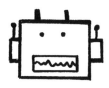 

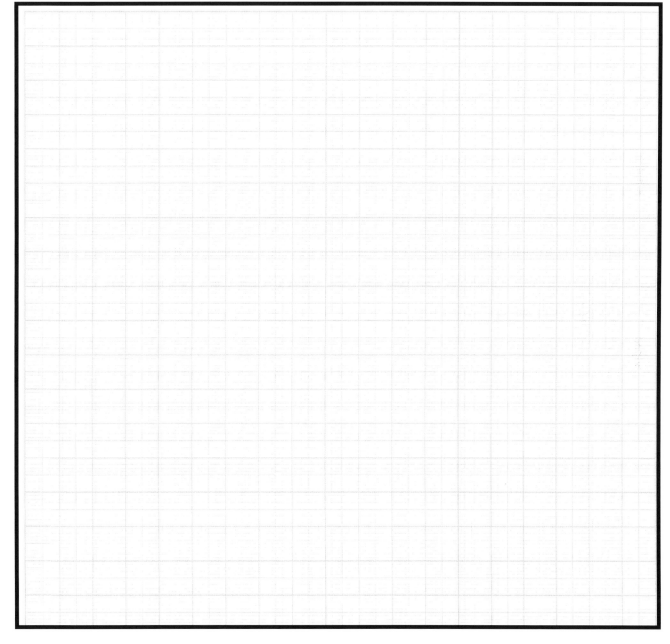

Uranus

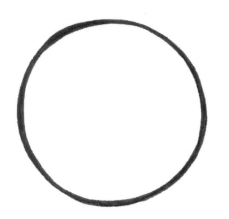

How many moons does
Uranus have?

_____

How many hours are
in 1 Uranus day?

_____

How many days
are in 1 Uranus
year?

_____

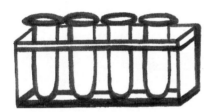

What is Uranus
made of?

_____

What is the temperature on Uranus?

_____

How much would you weigh if you were on Uranus?

_____

Write down **3** interesting facts about Uranus:

1._____
_____

2._____
_____

3._____
_____

DRAW YOUR OWN URANUS

WATCH A DOCUMENTARY ABOUT SPACE

Notes:

Ideas:

Rating:
AWFUL
BAD
LAME
YUCKY
OKAY
NICE
GOOD
GREAT
SUPER
AMAZING

Title:

Topic:

Use this space to doodle

INTERESTING FACTS ABOUT THIS DOCUMENTARY:

Draw a scene from the documentary:

Write a review:

INTERESTING FACTS ABOUT THIS DOCUMENTARY:

SPACE DISCOVERIES

CHOOSE A PERSON OR A TOPIC TO STUDY

(Astronauts, NASA Engineers, Astronomers, etc.)

Date:

Name:_____

_____

_____

_____

_____

_____

_____

_____

_____

_____

_____

_____

_____

_____

Draw a diagram or illustration:

NEWS FROM SPACE

WHAT WOULD YOU LIKE TO LEARN ABOUT SPACE?

_____

_____

_____

_____

_____

_____

_____

_____

DRAW THE CURRENT PHASE OF THE MOON

SPACE IN THE NEWS

FIND PAST OR CURRENT NEWS ARTICLES AND STORIES,
AND WRITE OR DRAW ABOUT THEM IN THIS SECTION

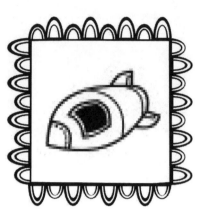

READING TIME

Today's Date:

_____

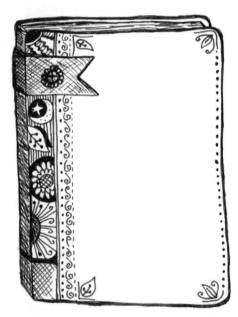

SET YOUR TIMER FOR 30 MINUTES!
READ UNTIL THE TIMER STOPS!

Date:

READING TIME

Copy an interesting paragraph
or list from your book.
Book Title:_____ **Page #**_____

_____
_____
_____
_____
_____
_____
_____
_____
_____
_____
_____
_____
_____
_____

Illustration

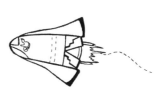

Neptune

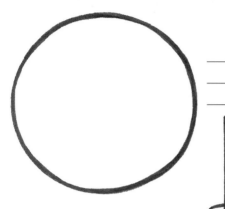

What is Neptune made of?

_____
_____
_____

How many moons does Neptune have?

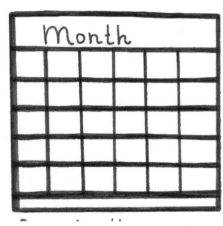

How many days are in **1** Neptune year?

How much would you weigh if you were on Neptune?

What is the temperature on Neptune?

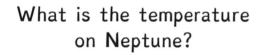

DRAW YOUR OWN NEPTUNE

SELECT A SPACE MISSION TO LEARN MORE ABOUT

The name of the mission:

_____

DATE:

_____

Write about this mission.
When and where did it take place? Who was involved?
How did it end?

_____

_____

_____

_____

_____

_____

_____

_____

_____

_____

_____

_____

_____

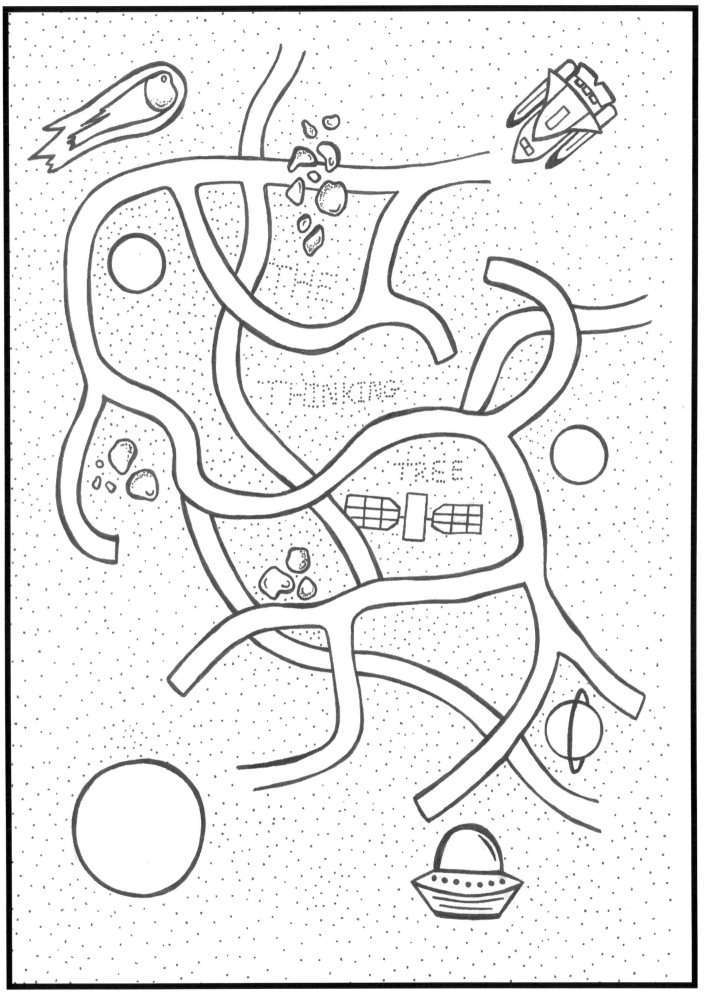

VOCABULARY BUILDING

Look in your Space Books
for **FOUR** words with more than **TEN** letters.
Write the words and their definitions below:

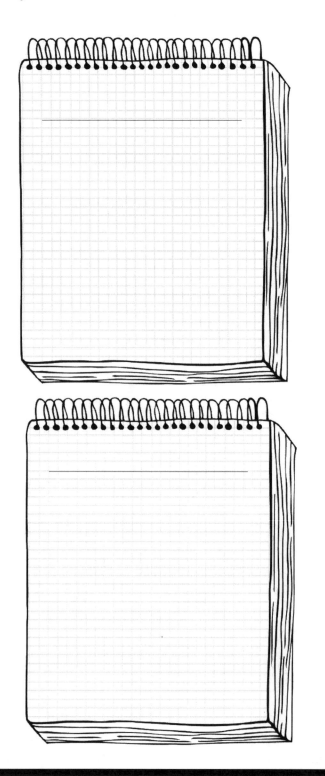

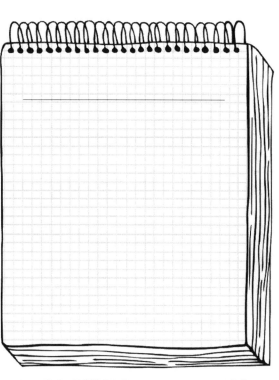

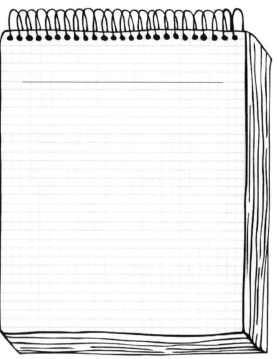

Spelling Time

Find 20 Words with 8 letters each.

Look in your books for words.

Write the words here:

_____   _____

_____   _____

_____   _____

_____   _____

_____   _____

_____   _____

_____   _____

_____   _____

_____   _____

_____   _____

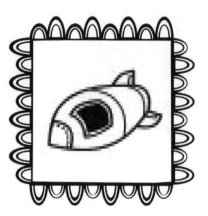

Spend Time reading your books!

Write and draw about what your learned!

Today's Date:
_____

READING TIME

SET YOUR TIMER FOR 30 MINUTES!
READ UNTIL THE TIMER STOPS!

Date:

READING TIME

Copy an interesting paragraph
or list from your book.

Book Title:_____ **Page #**_____

_____
_____
_____
_____
_____
_____
_____
_____
_____
_____
_____
_____
_____
_____

Illustration

Pluto

What is Pluto
made of?

_____
_____
_____
_____
_____
_____

What is the
temperature on
Pluto?

How many hours are
in **1** Pluto day?

_____

How many days are
in **1** Pluto year?

_____

How many moons does
Pluto have?

_____

Write down **3** interesting facts about Pluto:

1._____

2._____

3._____

QUESTION FOR DISCUSSION:
WHAT HAPPENED TO PLUTO?

DRAW YOUR OWN PLUTO

WATCH A DOCUMENTARY ABOUT SPACE

Notes:

Ideas:

Rating:
AWFUL
BAD
LAME
YUCKY
OKAY
NICE
GOOD
GREAT
SUPER
AMAZING

Title:

Topic:

Use this space to doodle

INTERESTING FACTS ABOUT THIS DOCUMENTARY:

_____
_____
_____
_____
_____

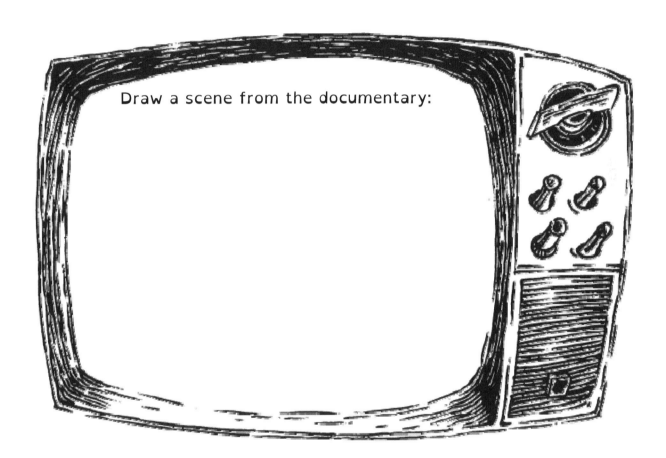

Draw a scene from the documentary:

Write a review:

_____
_____
_____
_____
_____

INTERESTING FACTS ABOUT THIS DOCUMENTARY:

CREATIVE WRITING

Names & Descriptions of Characters:

_____

_____

_____

_____

Title:

_____

_____

_____

_____

_____

_____

_____

_____

_____

_____

_____

_____

_____

_____

_____

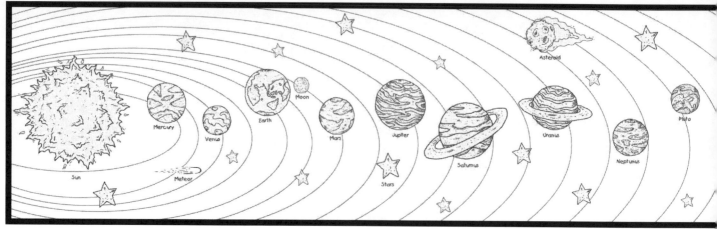

COMPLETE THE SOLAR SYSTEM

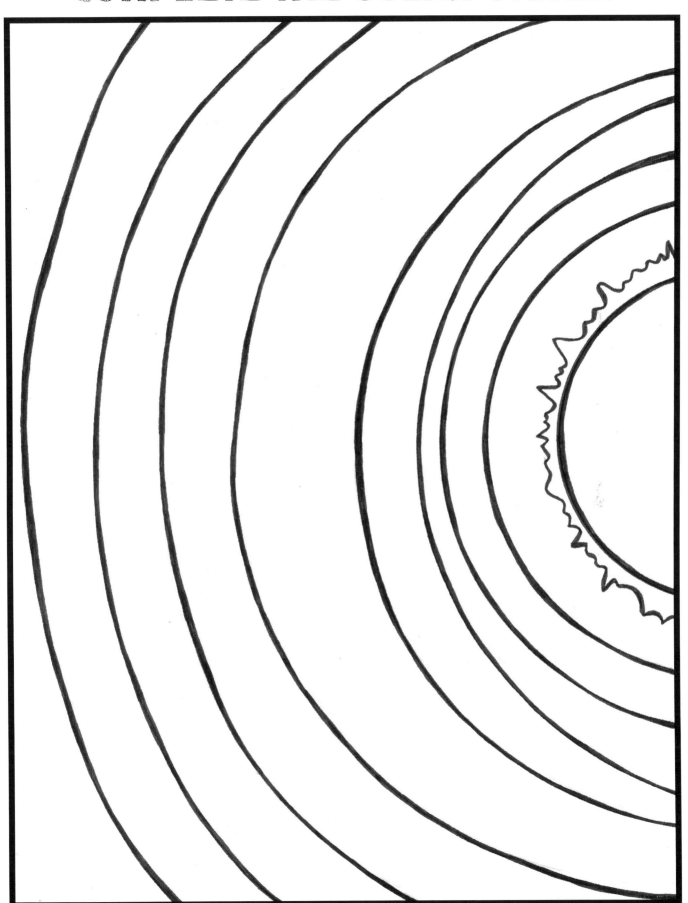

FIND THE DISTANCE

Materials:

A roll of toilet paper, picture of each planet

Instructions:

Find the distance of each planet from the Sun.
Use a calculator to figure out how many pieces
of toilet paper you need for each planet.
1 square of toilet paper = 57,910,000 km
First piece of toilet paper represents the Sun;
you will start counting from the Sun.

LEARN ABOUT
THE LIFE CYCLE
OF A STAR

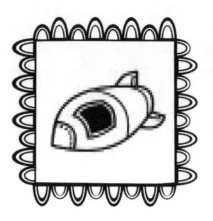

Spend Time reading your books!

Write and draw about what your learned!

READING TIME

Today's Date:

_____

SET YOUR TIMER FOR 30 MINUTES!
READ UNTIL THE TIMER STOPS!

Date: _____

READING TIME

Copy an interesting paragraph
or list from your book.

Book Title:_____ **Page #**_____

_____
_____
_____
_____
_____
_____
_____
_____
_____
_____
_____
_____
_____
_____

Illustration

DESIGN YOUR OWN ROBOT

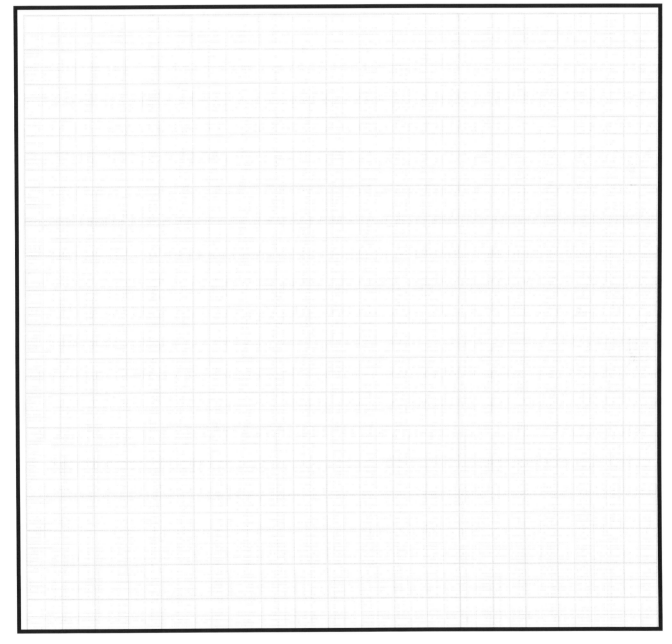

LEARN ABOUT
EARTH'S ROTATION

_____
_____
_____
_____
_____
_____
_____
_____
_____
_____
_____
_____
_____
_____
_____
_____

CREATE A PLANET

NEWS FROM SPACE

WHAT WOULD YOU LIKE TO LEARN ABOUT SPACE?

_____

_____

_____

_____

_____

_____

_____

_____

DRAW THE CURRENT PHASE OF THE MOON

SPACE IN THE NEWS
FIND PAST OR CURRENT NEWS ARTICLES AND STORIES, AND WRITE OR DRAW ABOUT THEM IN THIS SECTION

COLOR AND FINISH THIS PICTURE

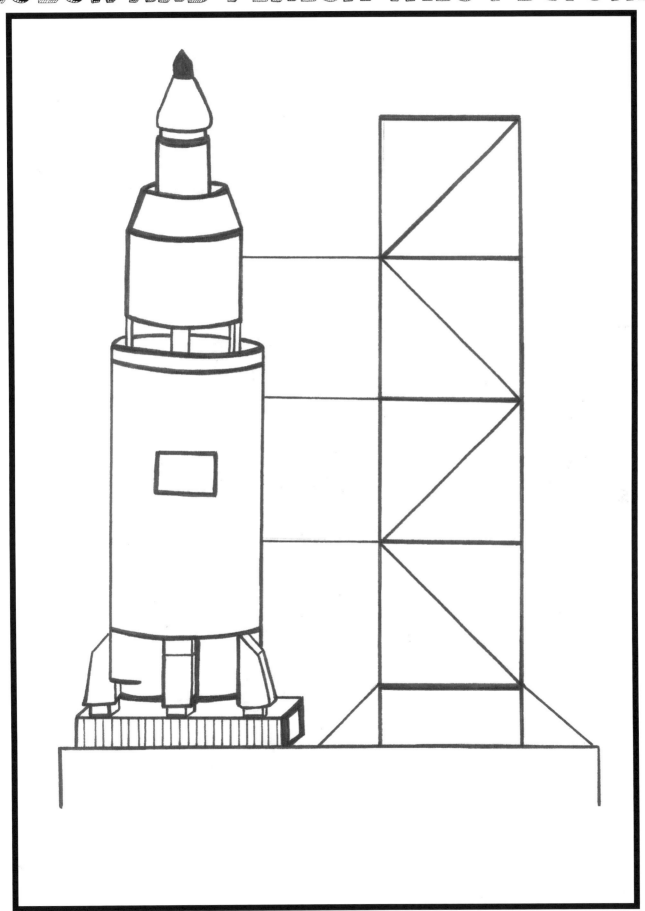

CREATIVE WRITING

Names & Descriptions of Characters:

_____
_____
_____
_____

Title:

_____

_____
_____
_____
_____
_____
_____
_____
_____
_____
_____
_____
_____
_____
_____
_____

SPACE DISCOVERIES
CHOOSE A PERSON OR A TOPIC TO STUDY
(Astronauts, NASA Engineers, Astronomers, etc.)

Name:_____

_____
_____
_____
_____
_____
_____
_____
_____
_____
_____
_____
_____
_____

Draw a diagram or illustration:

SCIENCE PROJECT:
Projection Box

Materials:

box, scissors, flashlight, tape, hole punch,
index cards, and toothpicks

  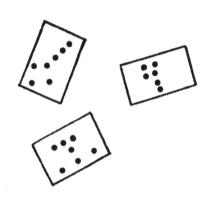

Instructions:

Cut a large hole in one end of the box (the index card will go over this).

Cut a flashlight-sized hole in the other end of the box
(the flashlight should cover the hole without going in the hole).

Make sure all other cracks and holes are covered.

Draw constellations on the index cards. Use the hole punch for the
large stars and the toothpicks to make holes for the smaller stars.

Cover the larger hole with one index card at a time.

Shine the flashlight through the other end, pointing your projector
at a wall or other flat surface.

DISCOVERING CONSTELLATIONS AND THEIR MEANINGS

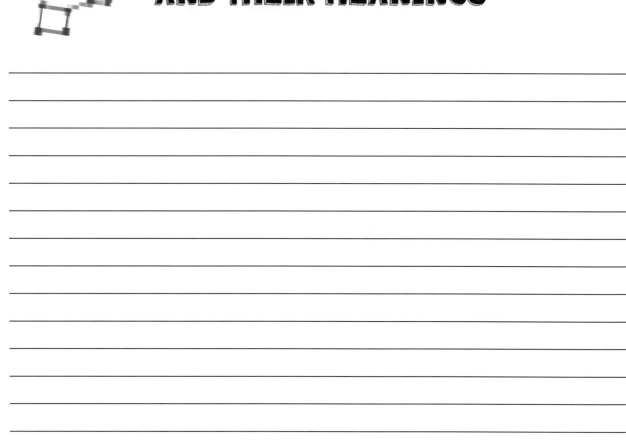

_____
_____
_____
_____
_____
_____
_____
_____
_____
_____
_____
_____
_____

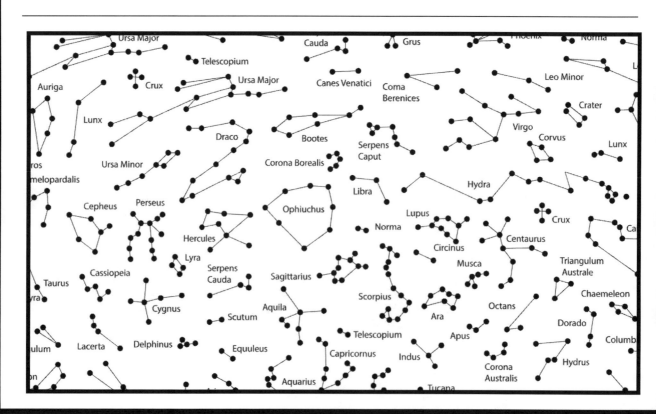

DRAW YOUR FAVORITE CONSTELLATIONS

FIND THE CONSTELLATIONS

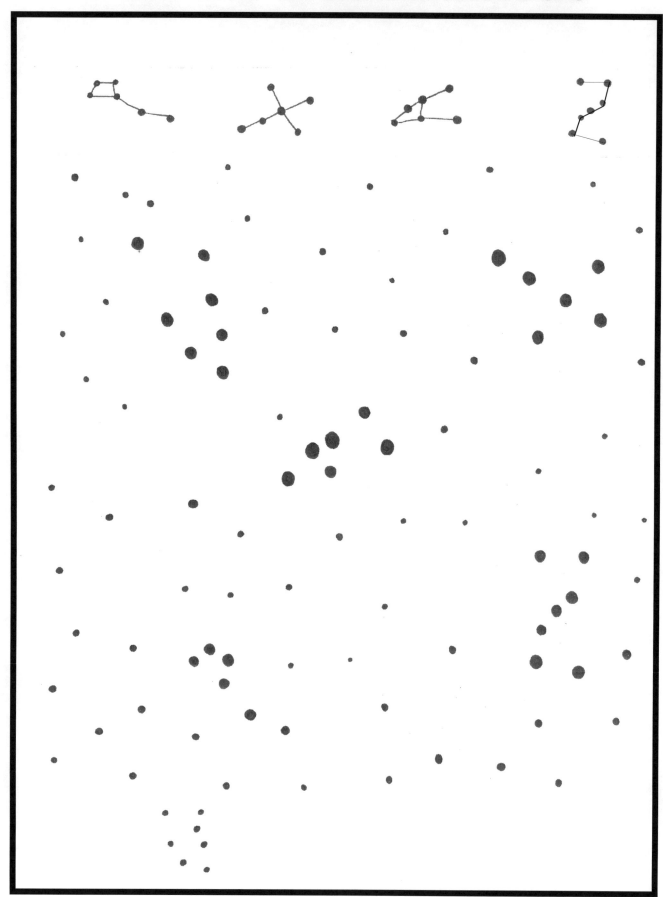

FIND THE CONSTELLATIONS

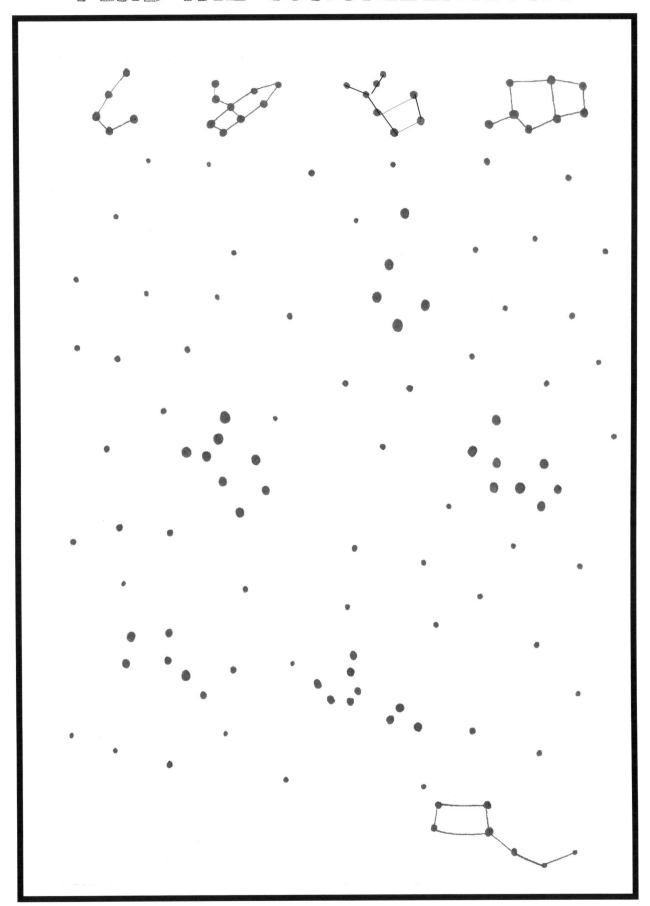

VOCABULARY BUILDING

Look in your Space Books
for **FOUR** words with more than **TEN** letters.
Write the words and their definitions below:

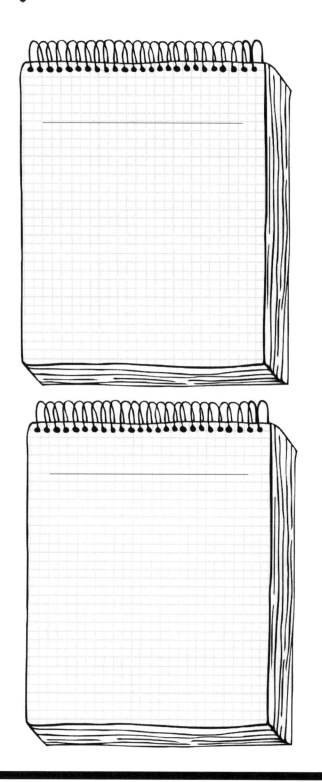

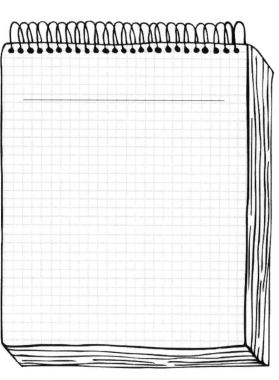

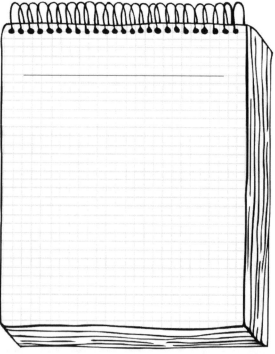

Spelling Time

Find 20 Words with 7 letters each.

Look in your books for words.

Write the words here:

_____   _____

_____   _____

_____   _____

_____   _____

_____   _____

_____   _____

_____   _____

_____   _____

_____   _____

_____   _____

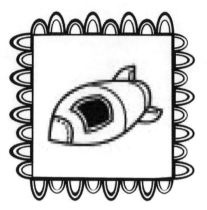

Spend Time reading your books!

Write and draw about what your learned!

Today's Date:

_____

READING TIME

SET YOUR TIMER FOR 30 MINUTES!
READ UNTIL THE TIMER STOPS!

Date:

READING TIME

Copy an interesting paragraph
or list from your book.

Book Title:_____ **Page #**_____

_____
_____
_____
_____
_____
_____
_____
_____
_____
_____
_____
_____
_____
_____

Illustration

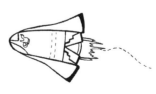

COLOR AND FINISH THIS PICTURE

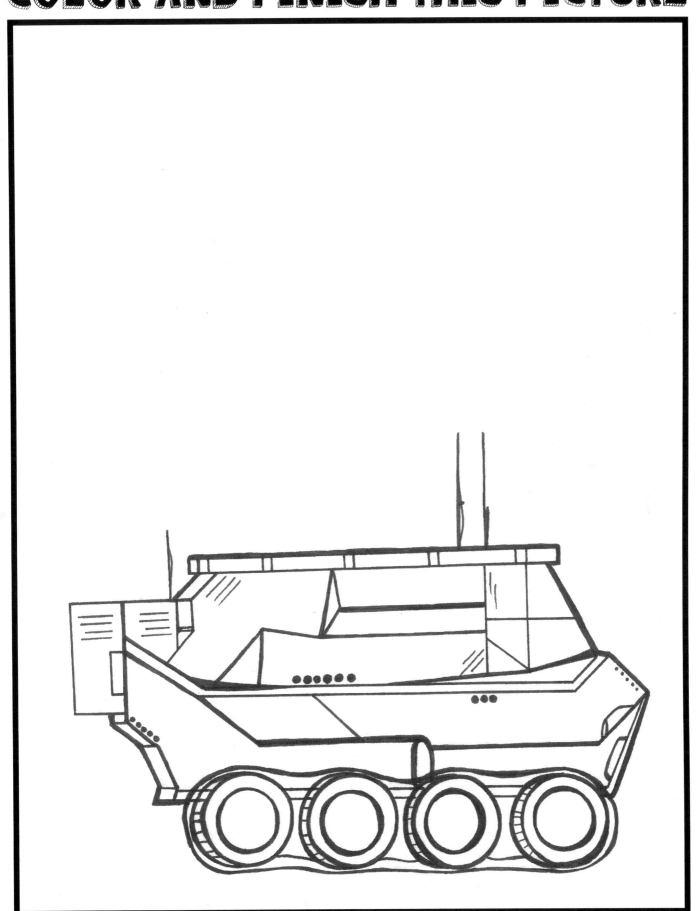

NEWS FROM SPACE

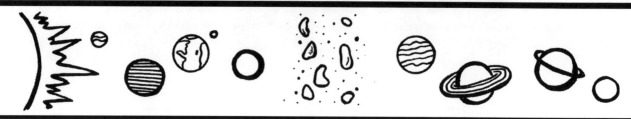

WHAT WOULD YOU LIKE TO LEARN ABOUT SPACE?

_____

_____

_____

_____

_____

_____

_____

_____

DRAW THE CURRENT PHASE OF THE MOON

SPACE IN THE NEWS
FIND PAST OR CURRENT NEWS ARTICLES AND STORIES, AND WRITE OR DRAW ABOUT THEM IN THIS SECTION

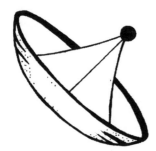

SCIENCE PROJECT:
Constructing Constellations

Materials:

Pictures of constellations,
mini marshmallows,
and toothpicks

Instructions:

Use the marshmallows and toothpicks
to construct constellations.

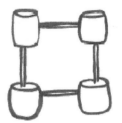

DRAW THE RESULTS

COMETS VS. METEORS

CREATE YOUR OWN
SPACECRAFT

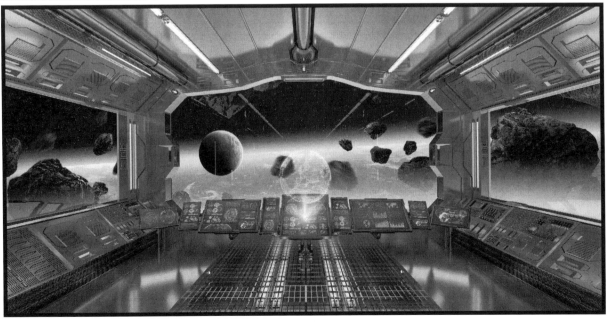

CREATIVE WRITING

Names & Descriptions of Characters:

_____

_____

_____

_____

_____

Title:

_____

_____

_____

_____

_____

_____

_____

_____

_____

_____

_____

_____

_____

_____

_____

_____

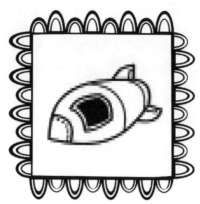

READING TIME

Today's Date:

_____

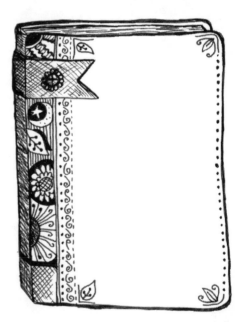

SET YOUR TIMER FOR 30
MINUTES!
READ UNTIL THE TIMER STOPS!

READING TIME

Copy an interesting paragraph
or list from your book.

Book Title:_____ **Page #**_____

_____
_____
_____
_____
_____
_____
_____
_____
_____
_____
_____
_____
_____
_____

Date:

Illustration

MY SPACE DRAWINGS AND NOTES

SCIENCE PROJECT:
Build your own
Refracting Telescope

Materials:

Two magnifying glasses – perhaps **1–1.5** inches (**2.5–3 cm**) diameter
(it works best if one is larger than the other).
A cardboard tube, duct tape, scissors, a ruler, yard stick
or tape measure, newspaper or magazine.

Instructions:

1. Take the two magnifying glasses and newspaper. Hold one magnifying glass (the bigger one) between you and the paper. The image of the print will look blurry.

2. Place the second magnifying glass between your eye and the first magnifying glass. Move the second glass forward or backward until the print comes into sharp focus. You will notice that the print appears larger and upside down.

3. Measure the distance between the two magnifying glasses and write the distance down. (You might need to ask someone to help with this step.)

4. Cut a slot in the cardboard tube about an inch away from the front opening. Do not cut all the way through the tube. The slot should be able to hold the large magnifying glass.

5. Cut another slot in the tube the same distance from the first slot (what you wrote down in **Step 3**). This is where the second magnifying glass will go.

6. Place the two magnifying glasses in their slots (big one at front, little one at back) and tape them in place with the duct tape.

7. Leave about **0.5–1** inch of tube behind the small magnifying glass and trim any remaining tube.

8. Check to see that it works by looking at the printed page. You may have to make slight adjustments to get the exact distances between the two glasses right so that the image comes into focus.

WATCH A DOCUMENTARY ABOUT SPACE

Notes:

Ideas:

Rating:
AWFUL
BAD
LAME
YUCKY
OKAY
NICE
GOOD
GREAT
SUPER
AMAZING

Title:

Topic:

Use this space to doodle

INTERESTING FACTS ABOUT THIS DOCUMENTARY:

_____

_____

_____

_____

_____

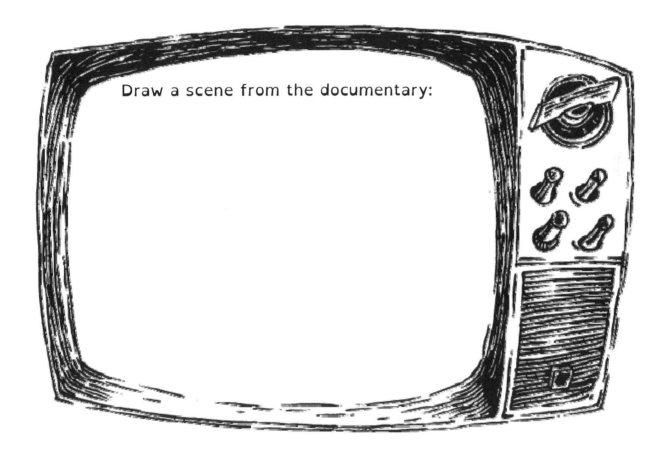

Draw a scene from the documentary:

Write a review:

_____

_____

_____

_____

_____

ADD DRAWINGS AND EVENTS TO THE SPACE TIMELINE

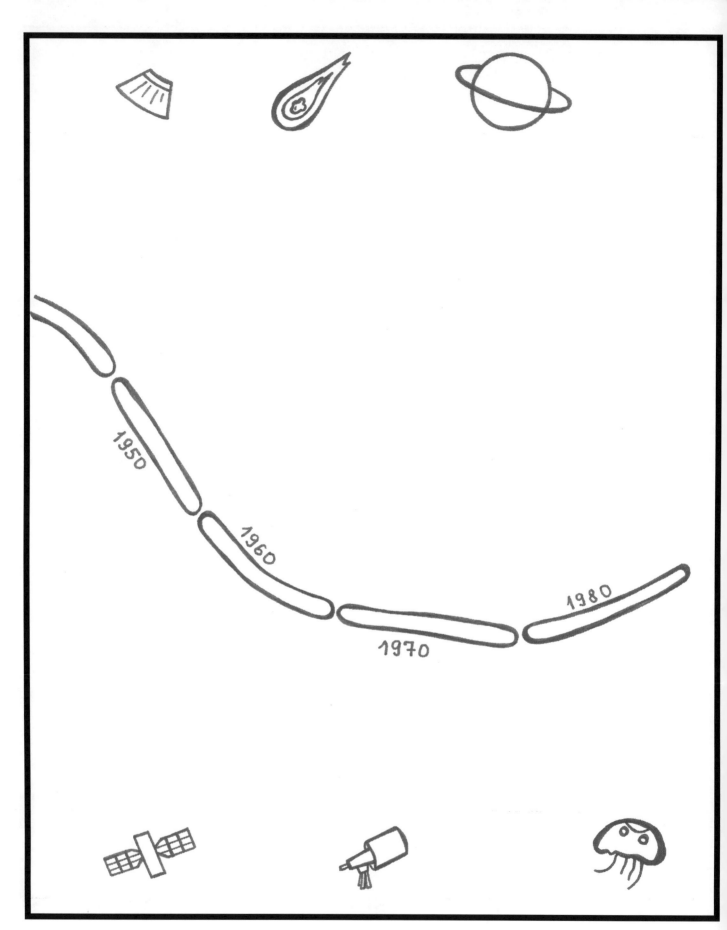

ADD DRAWINGS AND EVENTS TO THE SPACE TIMELINE

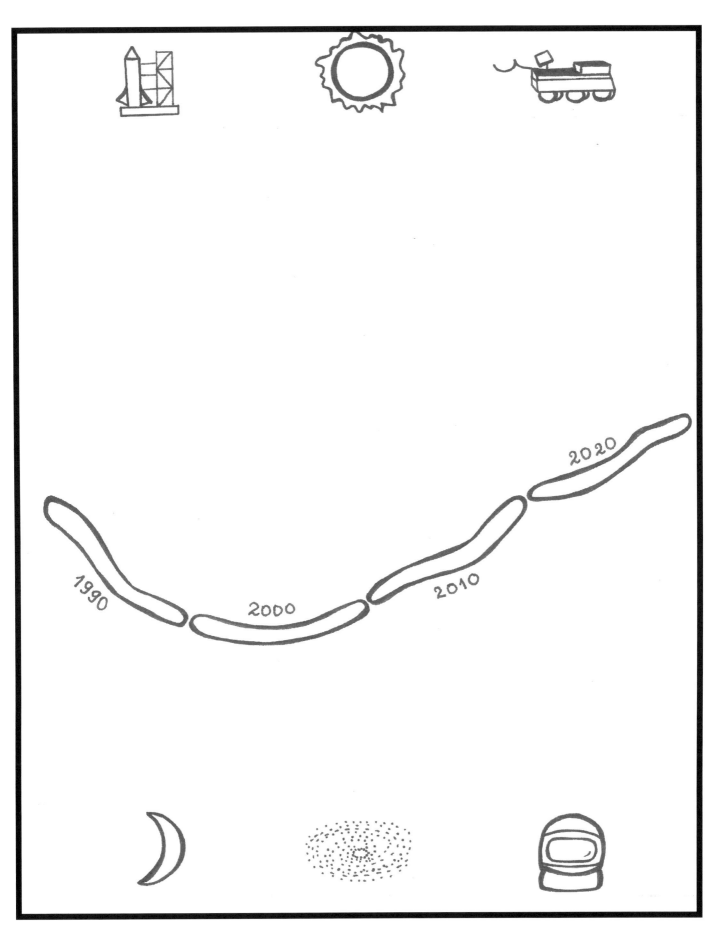

NEWS FROM SPACE

WHAT WOULD YOU LIKE TO LEARN ABOUT SPACE?

_____

_____

_____

_____

_____

_____

_____

_____

DRAW THE CURRENT PHASE OF THE MOON

SPACE IN THE NEWS

FIND PAST OR CURRENT NEWS ARTICLES AND STORIES, AND WRITE OR DRAW ABOUT THEM IN THIS SECTION

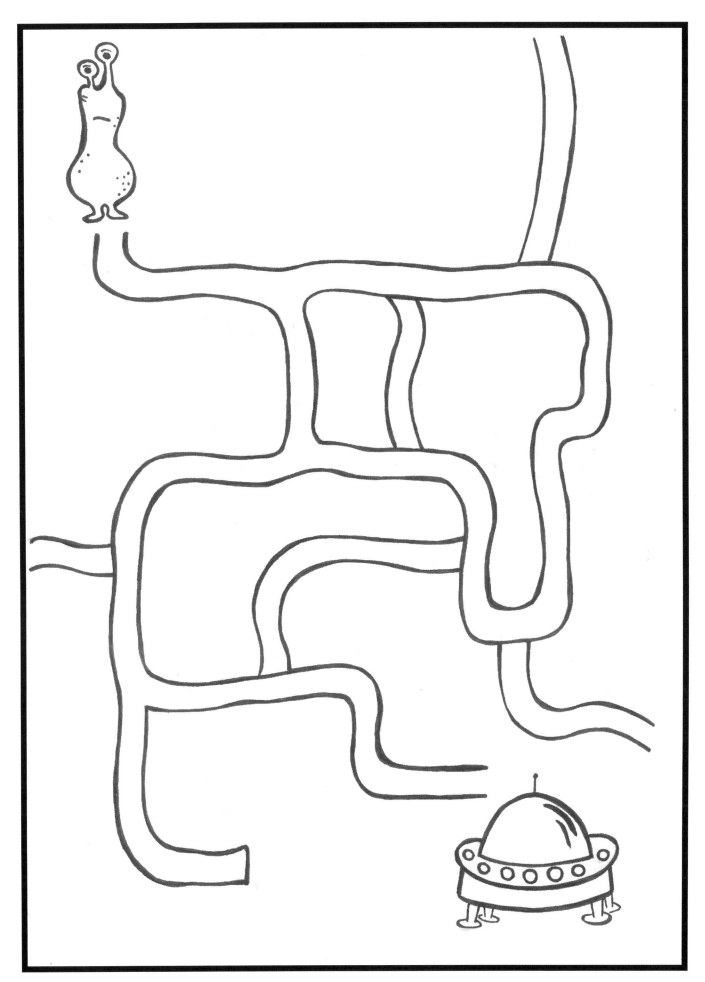

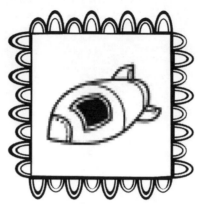

Spend Time
reading your
books!

Write and draw
about What your
Learned!

READING
TIME

Today's Date:

_____

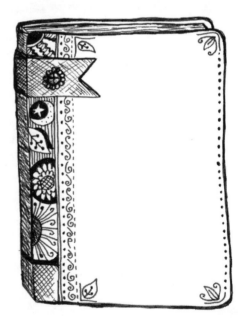

SET YOUR TIMER FOR 30
MINUTES!
READ UNTIL THE TIMER STOPS!

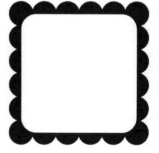

COLOR AND FINISH THIS PICTURE

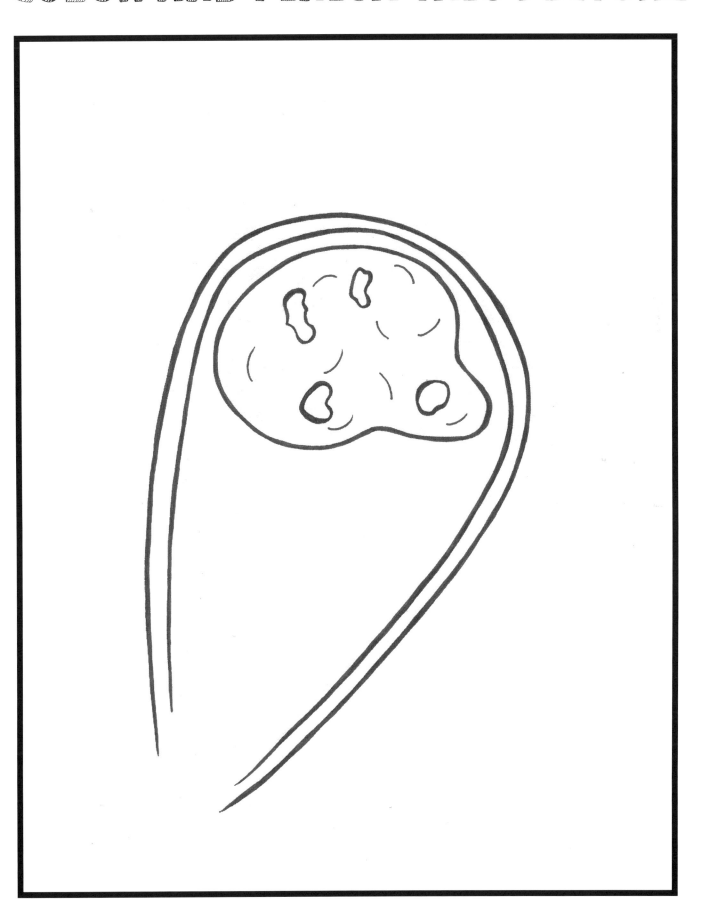

CREATIVE WRITING

Names & Descriptions of Characters:

_____
_____
_____
_____

Title:

_____

_____
_____
_____
_____
_____
_____
_____
_____
_____
_____
_____
_____
_____
_____
_____

SPACE DISCOVERIES

CHOOSE A PERSON OR A TOPIC TO STUDY

(Astronauts, NASA Engineers, Astronomers, etc.)

Name:_____

_____

_____

_____

_____

_____

_____

_____

_____

_____

_____

_____

_____

Draw a diagram or illustration:

SCIENCE PROJECT:
Landing Platform Challenge

Materials:

Rubber bands, index cards, cardboard, tape, Dixie cup, straws, and marshmallows.

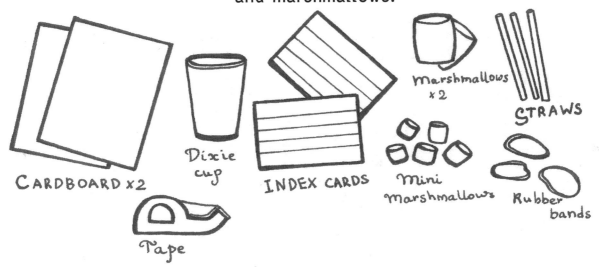

CARDBOARD x2   Dixie cup   INDEX CARDS   Marshmallows x2   STRAWS   Mini Marshmallows   Rubber bands   Tape

Instructions:

1. Use the tape, cardboard, index cards, rubber bands, and straws to build a landing platform.

2. Tape the cup in the middle of the top of your platform and place the marshmallows in the cup.

How high can you drop your platform
without it falling over
or bouncing out any marshmallows?

SELECT A SPACE MISSION TO LEARN MORE ABOUT

The name of the mission:

_____

DATE:

_____

Write about this mission.
When and where did it take place? Who was involved?
How did it end?

_____

_____

_____

_____

_____

_____

_____

_____

_____

_____

_____

_____

_____

NEWS FROM SPACE

WHAT WOULD YOU LIKE TO LEARN ABOUT SPACE?

_____
_____
_____
_____
_____
_____
_____
_____

DRAW THE CURRENT PHASE OF THE MOON

SPACE IN THE NEWS

FIND PAST OR CURRENT NEWS ARTICLES AND STORIES,
AND WRITE OR DRAW ABOUT THEM IN THIS SECTION

LEARN ABOUT
ASTRONAUTS

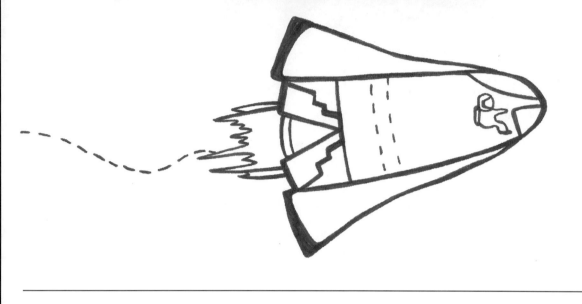

_____
_____
_____
_____
_____
_____
_____
_____
_____
_____
_____
_____
_____
_____
_____
_____
_____

HOW DO ASTRONAUTS TRAIN?

_____
_____
_____
_____
_____
_____
_____
_____
_____
_____
_____
_____
_____
_____

WATCH A DOCUMENTARY ABOUT SPACE

Notes:

Ideas:

Rating:
AWFUL
BAD
LAME
YUCKY
OKAY
NICE
GOOD
GREAT
SUPER
AMAZING

Title:

Topic:

Use this space to doodle

INTERESTING FACTS ABOUT THIS DOCUMENTARY:

_____

_____

_____

_____

_____

_____

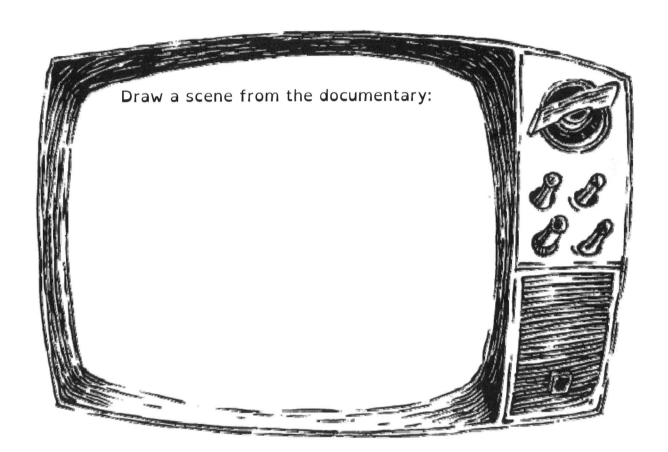

Draw a scene from the documentary:

Write a review:

_____

_____

_____

_____

_____

VOCABULARY BUILDING

Look in your Space Books
for **FOUR** words with more than **TEN** letters.
Write the words and their definitions below:

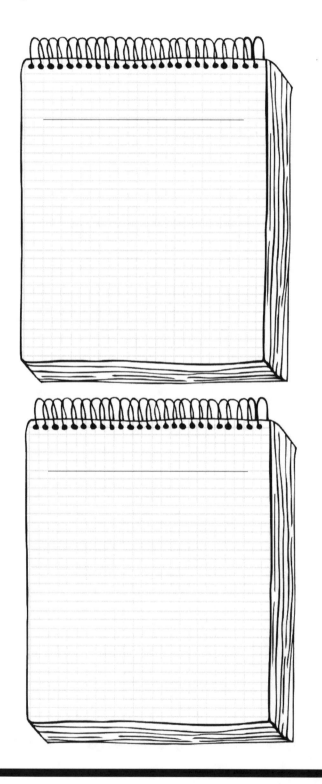

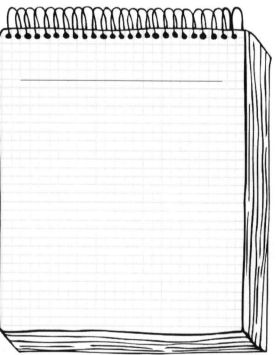

Spelling Time

Find 20 Words with 6 letters each.

Look in your books for words.

Write the words here:

_____   _____

_____   _____

_____   _____

_____   _____

_____   _____

_____   _____

_____   _____

_____   _____

_____   _____

_____   _____

COMPLETE THE SOLAR SYSTEM

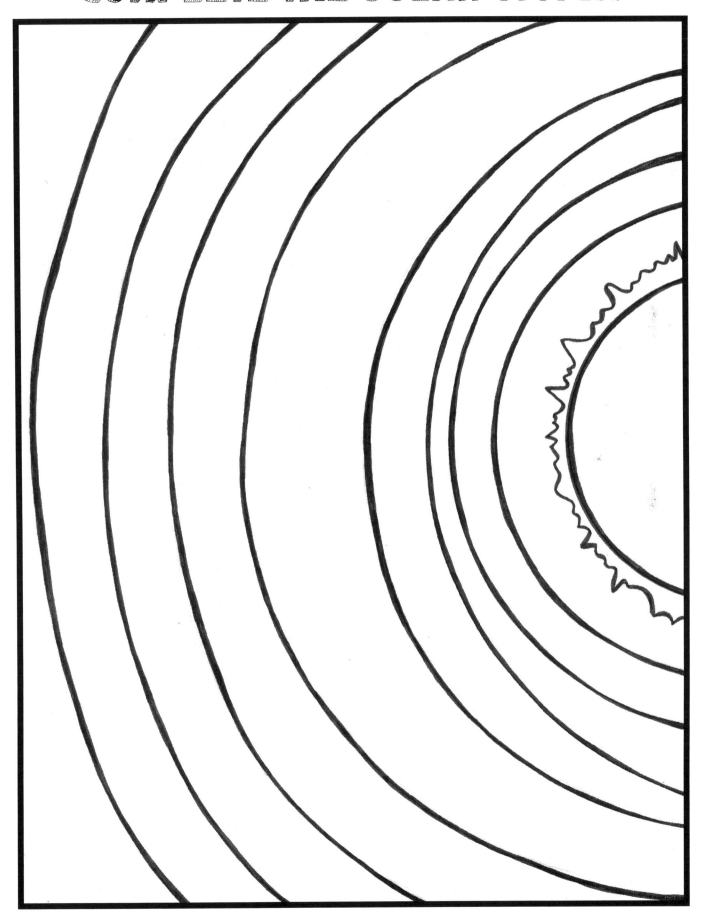

COLOR AND FINISH THIS PICTURE

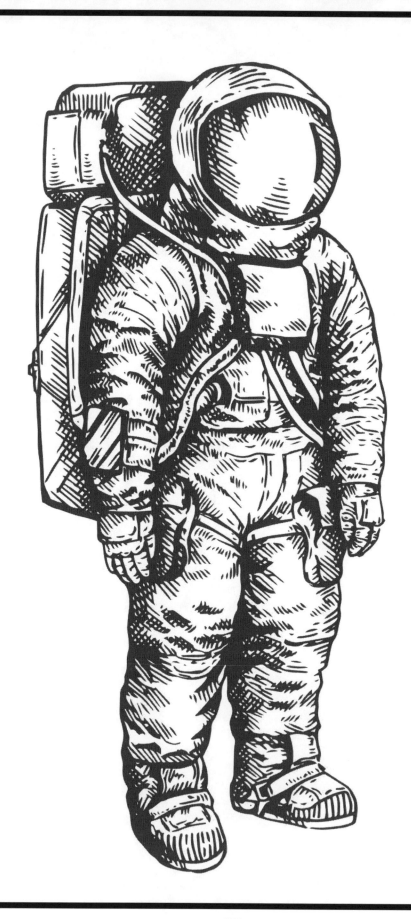

TRAINING EXERCISE

Supplies:

Kitchen rubber gloves or thick snow gloves, plastic wrap, box, screws, bolts, nuts, washers, other items that can be put together.

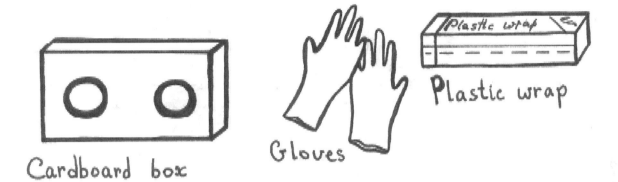

Cardboard box   Gloves   Plastic wrap

Instructions:

Cut holes in the sides of the box to put your hands through.
Put the gloves on, place your hands through the holes,
and try to assemble items.

DRAW A COMIC ABOUT YOUR EXPERIENCE

CREATIVE WRITING

Names & Descriptions of Characters:

_____

_____

_____

_____

Title:

_____

_____

_____

_____

_____

_____

_____

_____

_____

_____

_____

_____

_____

_____

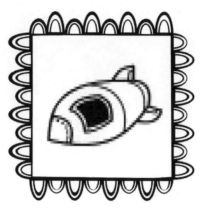

Today's Date:

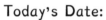

READING TIME

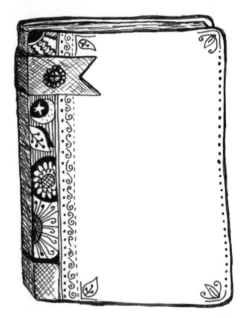

SET YOUR TIMER FOR 30 MINUTES!
READ UNTIL THE TIMER STOPS!

Date:

READING TIME

Copy an interesting paragraph
or list from your book.
Book Title:_____ **Page #_____**

_____
_____
_____
_____
_____
_____
_____
_____
_____
_____
_____
_____
_____
_____

Illustration

LEARN ABOUT
ANIMALS IN SPACE

_____

_____

_____

_____

_____

_____

_____

_____

_____

_____

_____

_____

_____

_____

_____

_____

_____

_____

_____

_____

_____

_____

NEWS FROM SPACE

WHAT WOULD YOU LIKE TO LEARN ABOUT SPACE?

_____
_____
_____
_____
_____
_____
_____

DRAW THE CURRENT PHASE OF THE MOON

SPACE IN THE NEWS
FIND PAST OR CURRENT NEWS ARTICLES AND STORIES, AND WRITE OR DRAW ABOUT THEM IN THIS SECTION

CREATE YOUR OWN
SPACESHIP

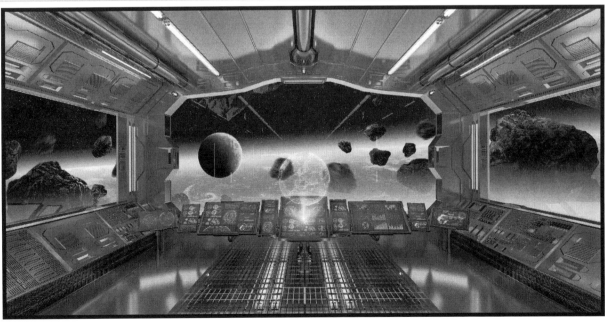

SPACE DISCOVERIES

Date:

CHOOSE A PERSON OR A TOPIC TO STUDY

(Astronauts, NASA Engineers, Astronomers, etc.)

Name:

_____

_____

_____

_____

_____

_____

_____

_____

_____

_____

_____

_____

Draw a diagram or illustration:

BLAST OFF!

Supplies:

Items to create a launch platform (recyclables, blocks, Legos ...)
Empty 2-liter bottle, ¾-1 cup of vinegar, 1 tablespoon of baking soda, small square of paper towel, cork.

Instructions:

(Ask parents or teachers to supervise)
Pour vinegar into the 2-liter bottle.

Place baking soda on the paper towel and fold it up.

Stick the paper towel in the bottle, seal with the cork.

Turn it over and set it in the launch pad.

BACK UP!

Adjust your ingredients and see how high you can soar!

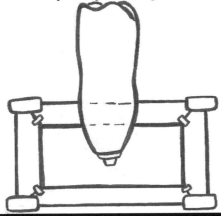

COLOR AND FINISH THIS PICTURE

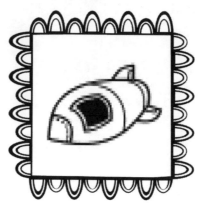

READING TIME

Today's Date:

_____

SET YOUR TIMER FOR 30 MINUTES!
READ UNTIL THE TIMER STOPS!

READING TIME

Copy an interesting paragraph
or list from your book.

Book Title:_____ **Page #**_____

Illustration

MY SPACE DRAWINGS AND NOTES

BUILD YOUR OWN

ROBOT

CD

Wire

Dome shaped
lid

AAA
batteries
x 2

Googly eyes

AAA Battery
holder

Switch

pencil with eraser

Supplies:

Blank/unwanted **CD**, dome-shaped lid
from Slurpie or similar drink
2 "AAA" battery holders
2 "AAA" batteries
1.5-3 V DC Motor, SPST (single pole single throw)
switch (be sure it's labeled push-on/push-off)
Short piece of wire (**22 gauge**)
Pencil with eraser
2 googly eyes (optional)

Tools:

Wire cutters, wire strippers, needle-nose pliers,
hot glue gun, electrical tape,
X-acto knife, cardboard, scissors.

Instructions:

Cut a piece of wire, 3-4 inches long.
Use the wire strippers to pull the outer layer off the wire (1/2 inch on each end).
Use the needle-nose pliers to bend the ends of the short wire to make it easier
to attach the wire to the motor and switch.
Use the needle-nose pliers to bend one end of the wire around one of the motor's
leads and the other end of the wire around one of the switch's leads.
Use the same technique to connect one of the wires coming from the battery pack
to the motor's free lead and the other wire coming from the battery pack to the
switch's free lead.
You should end up with your **3** components (motor, switch, battery pack) in a big circle.
It doesn't matter which order or orientation the pieces are in.
Cut the eraser off of the pencil and push the eraser onto the motor.
Hot glue the motor onto the **CD** with the eraser sticking through the hole.
Tape the battery pack to the motor and the **CD**.
Tape the dome lid over the motor and battery pack with the switch sticking
through the hole in the top.
Glue on some googly eyes (optional).

VOCABULARY BUILDING

Look in your Space Books
for **FOUR** words with more than **TEN** letters.
Write the words and their definitions below:

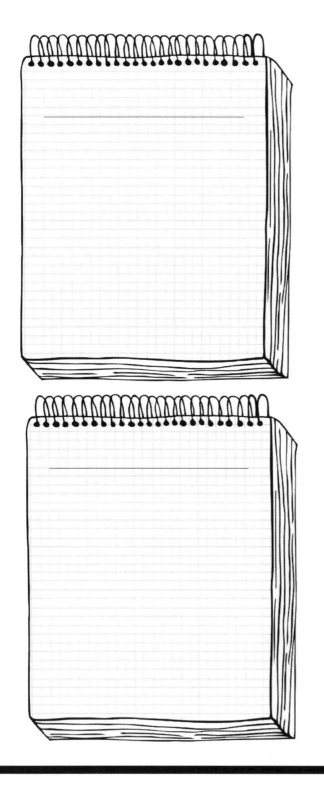

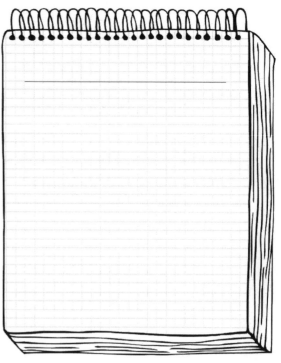

Spelling Time

Find 20 Words with 5 letters each.

Look in your books for words.

Write the words here:

_____   _____

_____   _____

_____   _____

_____   _____

_____   _____

_____   _____

_____   _____

_____   _____

_____   _____

SELECT A SPACE MISSION TO LEARN MORE ABOUT

The name of the mission:

_____

DATE:

_____

Write about this mission.
When and where did it take place? Who was involved?
How did it end?

_____

_____

_____

_____

_____

_____

_____

_____

_____

_____

_____

_____

_____

_____

LEARN ABOUT
BLACK HOLES

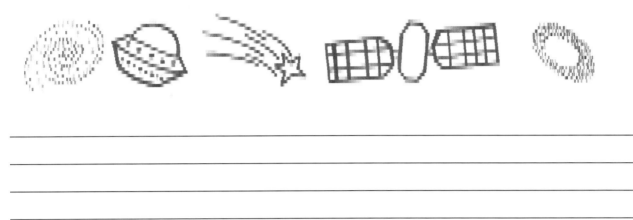

_____
_____
_____
_____
_____
_____
_____
_____
_____

DESIGN YOUR OWN
SPACE STATION

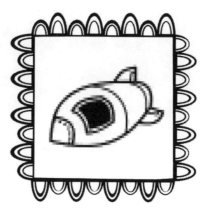

Spend Time reading your books!

Write and draw about what your Learned!

Today's Date:

_____

READING TIME

SET YOUR TIMER FOR 30 MINUTES!
READ UNTIL THE TIMER STOPS!

Date:

READING TIME

Copy an interesting paragraph
or list from your book.
Book Title:_____ **Page #_____**

_____
_____
_____
_____
_____
_____
_____
_____
_____
_____
_____
_____
_____
_____

Illustration

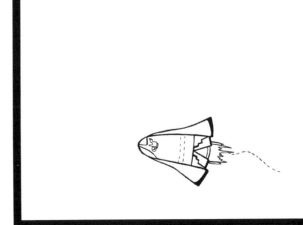

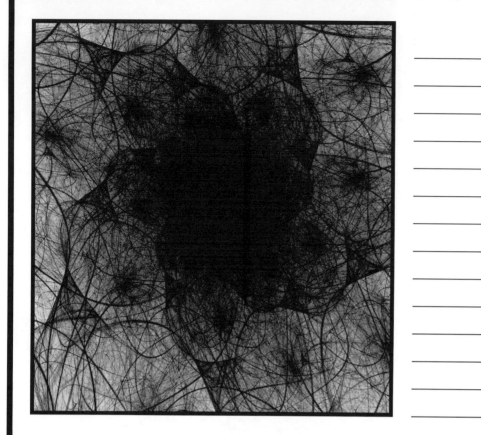

_____
_____
_____
_____
_____
_____
_____
_____
_____
_____
_____
_____
_____
_____

DARK ENERGY VS. DARK MATTER

_____
_____
_____
_____
_____
_____
_____
_____
_____
_____
_____
_____
_____

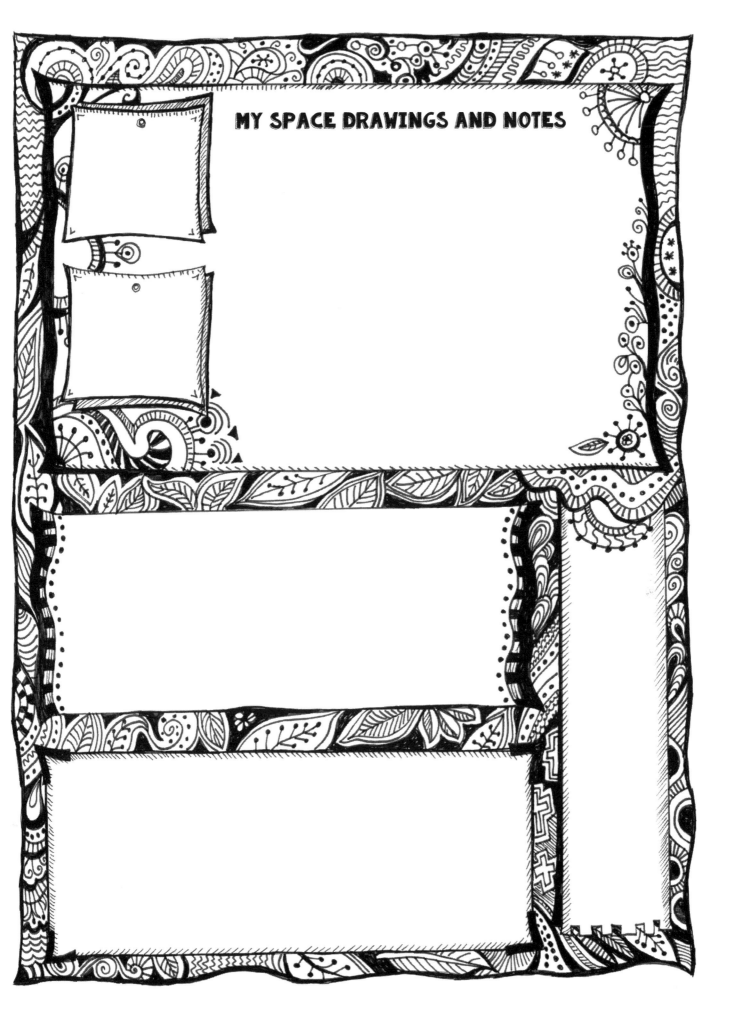

MY SPACE DRAWINGS AND NOTES

SPACE DISCOVERIES

CHOOSE A PERSON OR A TOPIC TO STUDY

(Astronauts, NASA Engineers, Astronomers, etc.)

Date:

Name: _____

_____

_____

_____

_____

_____

_____

_____

_____

_____

_____

_____

_____

Draw a diagram or illustration:

LEARN ABOUT
THE SPEED OF LIGHT

_____
_____
_____
_____
_____
_____
_____
_____
_____
_____
_____

NEWS FROM SPACE

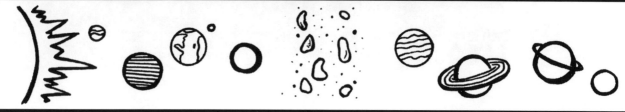

WHAT WOULD YOU LIKE TO LEARN ABOUT SPACE?

_____
_____
_____
_____
_____
_____
_____
_____

DRAW THE CURRENT PHASE OF THE MOON

SPACE IN THE NEWS
FIND PAST OR CURRENT NEWS ARTICLES AND STORIES, AND WRITE OR DRAW ABOUT THEM IN THIS SECTION

Date:

READING TIME

Copy an interesting paragraph
or list from your book.

Book Title:_____ **Page #**_____

_____
_____
_____
_____
_____
_____
_____
_____
_____
_____
_____
_____
_____
_____

Illustration

CREATIVE WRITING

Names & Descriptions of Characters:

_____

_____

_____

_____

Title:

_____

_____

_____

_____

_____

_____

_____

_____

_____

_____

_____

_____

_____

_____

LEARN ABOUT
THE WEATHER IN SPACE

Is there weather in space or on other planets?

_____

_____

_____

_____

_____

_____

_____

_____

_____

_____

_____

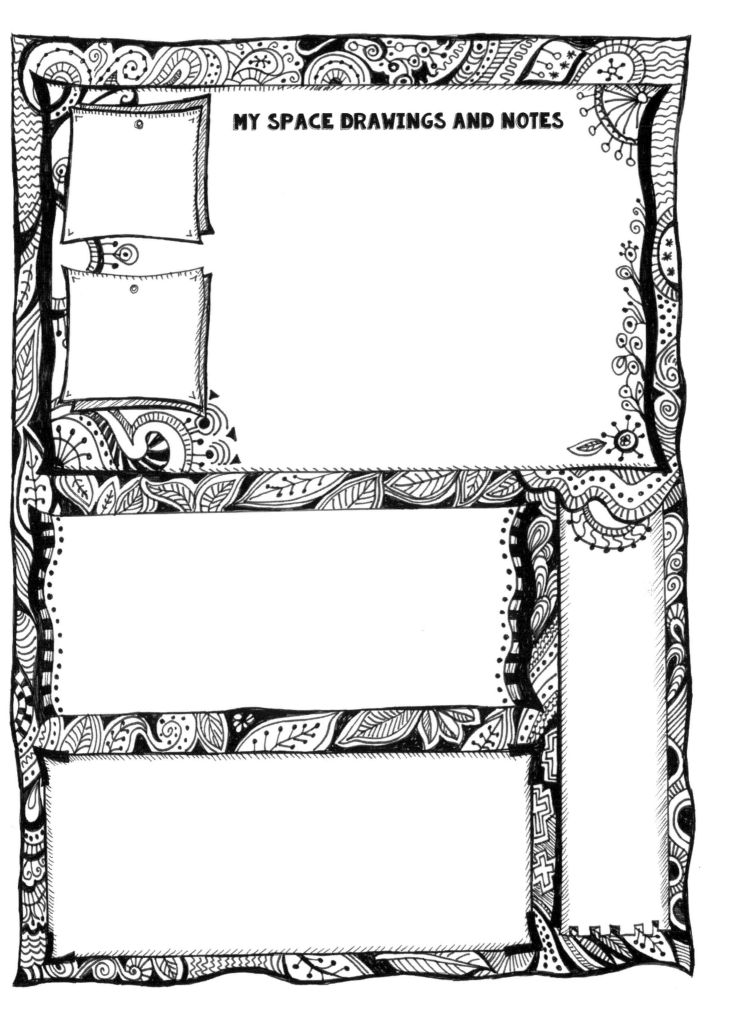

MY SPACE DRAWINGS AND NOTES

WATCH A DOCUMENTARY ABOUT SPACE

Notes:

Ideas:

Rating:
AWFUL
BAD
LAME
YUCKY
OKAY
NICE
GOOD
GREAT
SUPER
AMAZING

Title:

Topic:

Use this space to doodle

INTERESTING FACTS ABOUT THIS DOCUMENTARY:

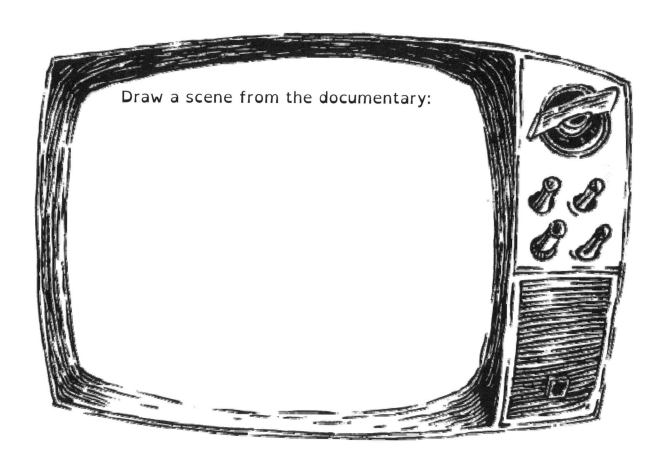

Draw a scene from the documentary:

Write a review:

COLOR AND FINISH THIS PICTURE

SELECT A SPACE MISSION TO LEARN MORE ABOUT

The name of the mission:

_____

DATE:

_____

Write about this mission.
When and where did it take place? Who was involved?
How did it end?

_____
_____
_____
_____
_____
_____
_____
_____
_____
_____
_____
_____
_____

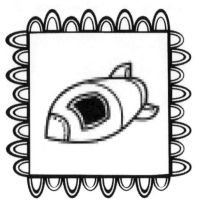

Spend Time reading your books!

Write and draw about What your Learned!

Today's Date:

_____

READING TIME

SET YOUR TIMER FOR 30 MINUTES!
READ UNTIL THE TIMER STOPS!

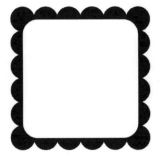

Date:

READING TIME

Copy an interesting paragraph
or list from your book.

Book Title:_____ **Page #**_____

_____
_____
_____
_____
_____
_____
_____
_____
_____
_____
_____
_____
_____
_____
_____

Illustration

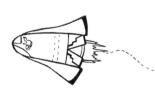

LEARN ABOUT
SPACE TRASH

What is it and where does it come from?

_____

_____

_____

_____

_____

_____

_____

_____

_____

_____

_____

_____

_____

_____

_____

_____

_____

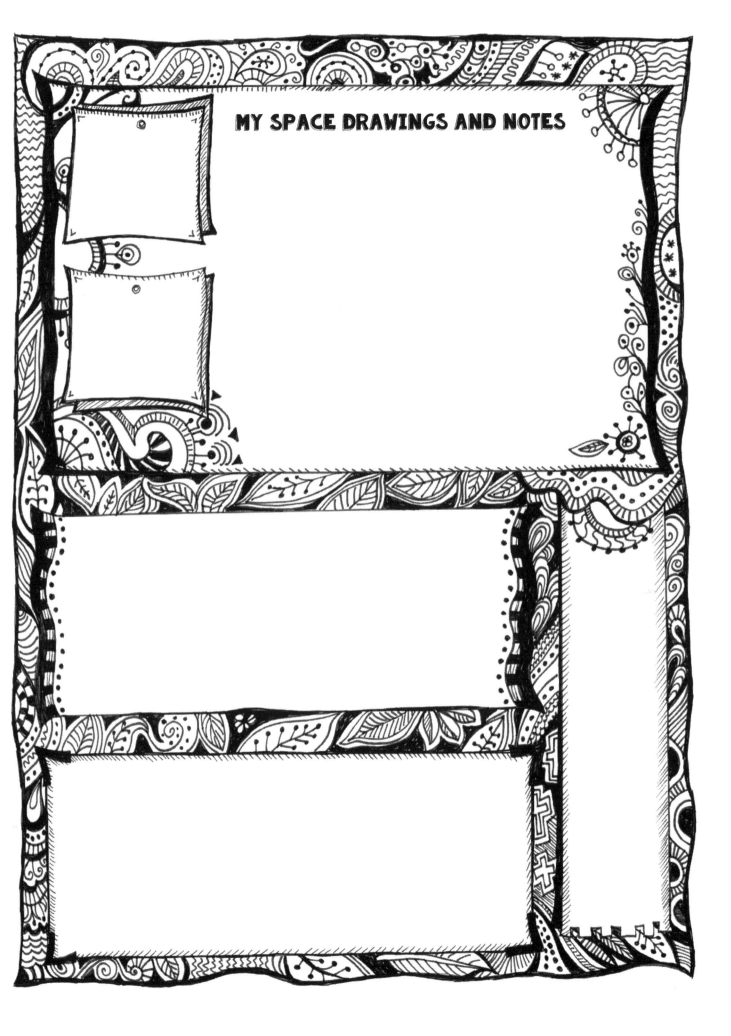

MY SPACE DRAWINGS AND NOTES

DESIGN YOUR OWN ROBOT

  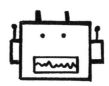 

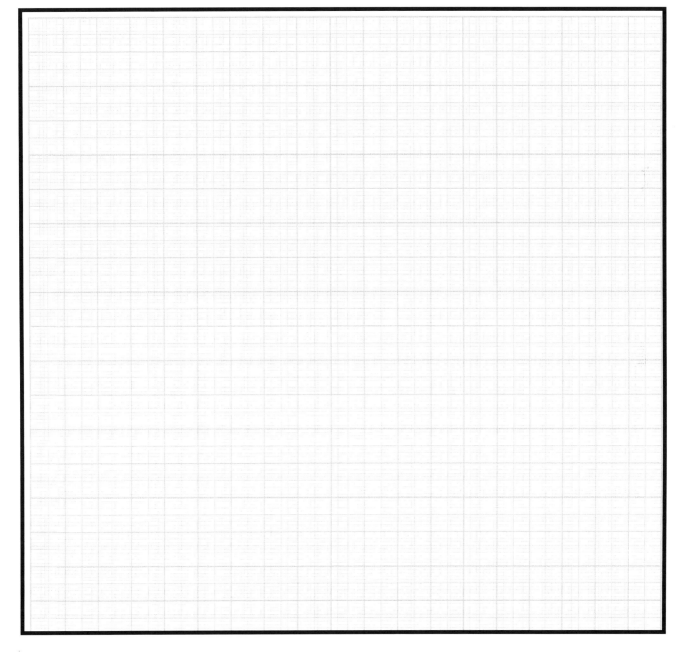

NEWS FROM SPACE

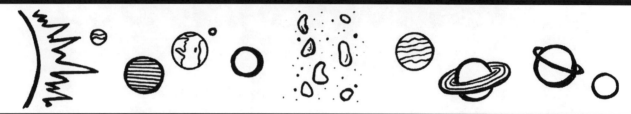

WHAT WOULD YOU LIKE TO LEARN ABOUT SPACE?

_____
_____
_____
_____
_____
_____
_____
_____

DRAW THE CURRENT PHASE OF THE MOON

SPACE IN THE NEWS

FIND PAST OR CURRENT NEWS ARTICLES AND STORIES,
AND WRITE OR DRAW ABOUT THEM IN THIS SECTION

SPACE DISCOVERIES
CHOOSE A PERSON OR A TOPIC TO STUDY
(Astronauts, NASA Engineers, Astronomers, etc.)

Date:

Name:_____

_____
_____
_____
_____
_____
_____
_____
_____
_____
_____
_____
_____

Draw a diagram or illustration:

WATCH A DOCUMENTARY ABOUT SPACE

Notes:

Ideas:

Rating:
AWFUL
BAD
LAME
YUCKY
OKAY
NICE
GOOD
GREAT
SUPER
AMAZING

Title:

Topic:

Use this space to doodle

INTERESTING FACTS ABOUT THIS DOCUMENTARY:

_____
_____
_____
_____
_____
_____

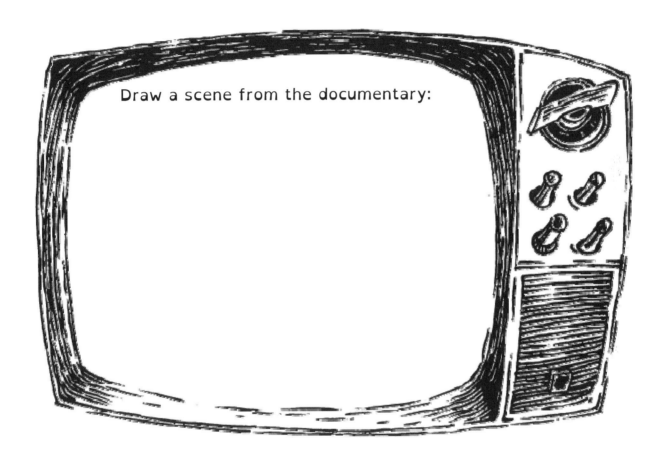

Draw a scene from the documentary:

Write a review:

_____
_____
_____
_____
_____

INTERESTING FACTS ABOUT THIS DOCUMENTARY:

CREATIVE WRITING

Names & Descriptions of Characters:

_____

_____

_____

_____

_____

Title:

_____

_____

_____

_____

_____

_____

_____

_____

_____

_____

_____

_____

_____

_____

_____

_____

CREATE A PLAN TO TRAVEL TO ANOTHER PLANET

Make a list of the things you
will take with you:

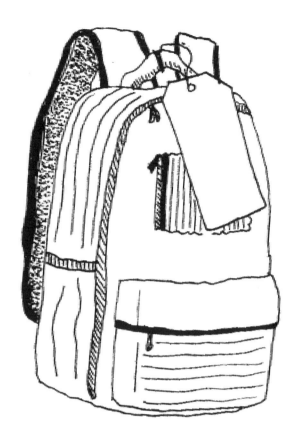

_____

_____

_____

_____

_____

_____

_____

_____

_____

_____

_____

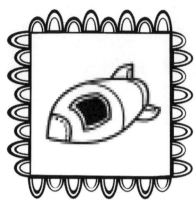

Today's Date:

_____

READING TIME

SET YOUR TIMER FOR 30 MINUTES!
READ UNTIL THE TIMER STOPS!

READING TIME

Copy an interesting paragraph
or list from your book.

Book Title:_____ **Page #**_____

Date:

_____
_____
_____
_____
_____
_____
_____
_____
_____
_____
_____
_____
_____

Illustration

COLOR AND FINISH THIS PICTURE

DRAW AN ILLUSTRATION ABOUT
WHAT IT IS LIKE TO LIVE ON THE SPACE STATION

WATCH A DOCUMENTARY ABOUT SPACE

Notes:

Ideas:

Rating:

AWFUL

BAD

LAME

YUCKY

OKAY

NICE

GOOD

GREAT

SUPER

AMAZING

Title:

Topic:

Use this space to doodle

INTERESTING FACTS ABOUT THIS DOCUMENTARY:

_____

_____

_____

_____

_____

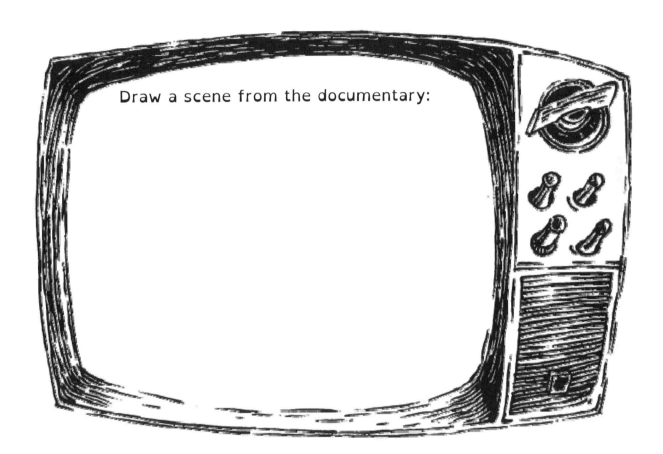

Draw a scene from the documentary:

Write a review:

_____

_____

_____

_____

_____

INTERESTING FACTS ABOUT THIS DOCUMENTARY:

CREATIVE WRITING

Names & Descriptions of Characters:

_____

_____

_____

_____

Title:

_____

_____

_____

_____

_____

_____

_____

_____

_____

_____

_____

_____

_____

_____

_____

_____

VOCABULARY BUILDING

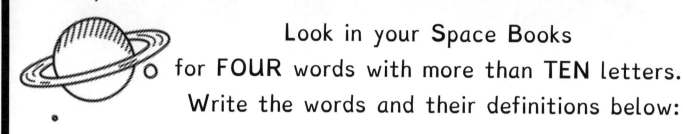

Look in your Space Books
for **FOUR** words with more than **TEN** letters.
Write the words and their definitions below:

Spelling Time

Find 20 Words with 8 letters each.

Look in your books for words.

Write the words here:

_____   _____

_____   _____

_____   _____

_____   _____

_____   _____

_____   _____

_____   _____

_____   _____

SELECT A SPACE MISSION TO LEARN MORE ABOUT

The name of the mission:

_____

DATE:

_____

Write about this mission.
When and where did it take place? Who was involved?
How did it end?

_____

_____

_____

_____

_____

_____

_____

_____

_____

_____

_____

_____

_____

_____

SPACE DISCOVERIES

CHOOSE A PERSON OR A TOPIC TO STUDY

(Astronauts, NASA Engineers, Astronomers, etc.)

Date:

Name:

Draw a diagram or illustration:

LEARN ABOUT
LIFE ON OTHER PLANETS

Could there be life on another planet?
What would it be like to live on another planet?
How would you survive?

_____
_____
_____
_____
_____
_____
_____
_____
_____
_____
_____

NEWS FROM SPACE

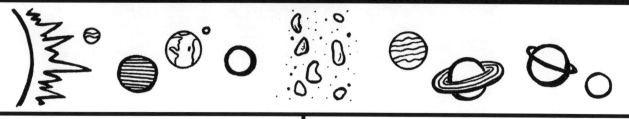

WHAT WOULD YOU LIKE TO LEARN ABOUT SPACE?

_____

_____

_____

_____

_____

_____

_____

_____

DRAW THE CURRENT PHASE OF THE MOON

SPACE IN THE NEWS

FIND PAST OR CURRENT NEWS ARTICLES AND STORIES, AND WRITE OR DRAW ABOUT THEM IN THIS SECTION

DESIGN YOUR OWN
SPACE COLONY

CREATIVE WRITING

Names & Descriptions of Characters:

_____

_____

_____

_____

_____

Title:

_____

_____

_____

_____

_____

_____

_____

_____

_____

_____

_____

_____

_____

_____

_____

_____

SPACE DISCOVERIES

Date:

CHOOSE A PERSON OR A TOPIC TO STUDY

(Astronauts, NASA Engineers, Astronomers, etc.)

Name:_____

_____

_____

_____

_____

_____

_____

_____

_____

_____

_____

_____

_____

_____

Draw a diagram or illustration:

MY SPACE DRAWINGS AND NOTES

WATCH A DOCUMENTARY ABOUT SPACE

Notes:

Ideas:

Rating:
AWFUL
BAD
LAME
YUCKY
OKAY
NICE
GOOD
GREAT
SUPER
AMAZING

Title:

Topic:

Use this space to doodle

INTERESTING FACTS ABOUT THIS DOCUMENTARY:

_____

_____

_____

_____

_____

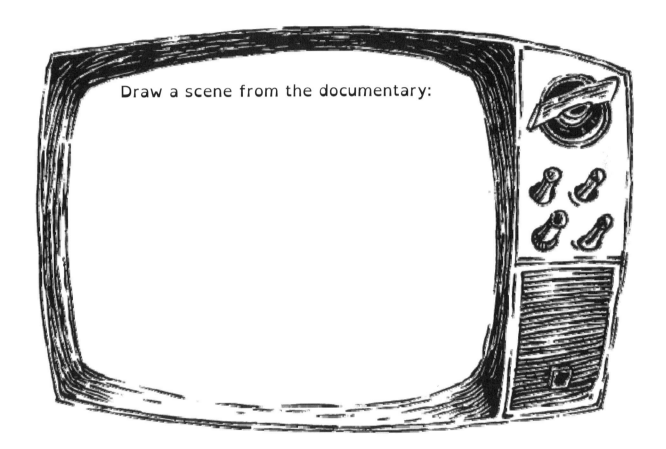

Draw a scene from the documentary:

Write a review:

_____

_____

_____

_____

_____

INTERESTING FACTS ABOUT THIS DOCUMENTARY:

NEWS FROM SPACE

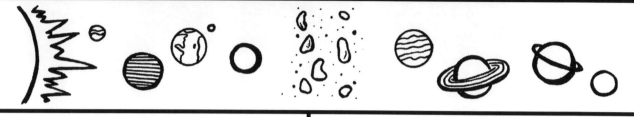

WHAT WOULD YOU LIKE TO LEARN ABOUT SPACE?

_____
_____
_____
_____
_____
_____
_____
_____

DRAW THE CURRENT PHASE OF THE MOON

SPACE IN THE NEWS
FIND PAST OR CURRENT NEWS ARTICLES AND STORIES, AND WRITE OR DRAW ABOUT THEM IN THIS SECTION

COLOR AND FINISH THIS PICTURE

LEARN ABOUT
THE THEORY OF RELATIVITY

_____
_____
_____
_____
_____
_____
_____
_____
_____
_____
_____
_____
_____
_____
_____
_____

_____
_____
_____
_____
_____
_____
_____
_____
_____
_____
_____
_____
_____

LEARN ABOUT
STRING THEORY

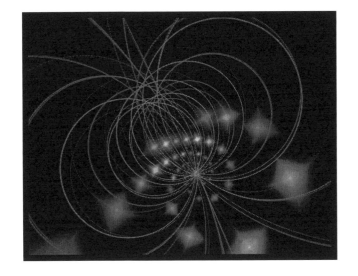

(blank ruled lines for notes)

$$G_{\mu\nu} = R_{\mu\nu} - \tfrac{1}{2}R g_{\mu\nu} = \frac{8\pi G}{c^4} T_{\mu\nu}$$

$$S_B = \frac{k_B\, 4\pi G}{\hbar c} M^2$$

$$\Psi_1(x) = \frac{1}{\sqrt{k_1}}\left(A_- e^{ikx} + A_- e^{ikx}\right) \quad x<0$$

$$k_1 = \sqrt{2mE/\hbar^2}$$

$$O = \frac{24\pi^3 L^2}{T^2 c^{-2}(1-e^2)}$$

$$R_{\mu\nu} - \tfrac{1}{2}R g_{\mu\nu} + \Lambda g_{\mu\nu} = \frac{8\pi G}{c^4} T_{\mu\nu}$$

$$H = \frac{PP}{2m} + V_{(r)}$$

$$Re[\Psi(x)] \qquad S = \frac{1}{2k}\int R\sqrt{-g}\, d^4x$$

$$S = \frac{c^3 kA}{4\hbar G}$$

$$P = -i\hbar\nabla$$

$$L = t_r\left\{\frac{1}{g^2}F_{1J}F^{1J} - i\lambda\,\Gamma^1 D_I\lambda\right\}$$

$$H|\Psi(t)\rangle = i\hbar\frac{\partial}{\partial t}|\Psi(t)\rangle$$

$$\frac{\delta(k_1+k_3)}{k_1^2}$$

$$E = mc^2$$
$$E^2 = (pc)^2 + (mc^2)^2$$

$$\Gamma = \frac{\theta}{2\pi} + \frac{4\pi}{g^2}$$

$$I = \int e^{-ax^2/2}dx = \sqrt{\frac{2\pi}{\alpha}}$$

$$E^2 = p^2c^2 + m^2c^4$$

$$\frac{1}{c^2}\frac{\partial^2}{\partial t^2}\Psi - \nabla^2\Psi + \frac{m^2c^2}{\hbar^2}\Psi = 0$$

$$P = \hbar k = \frac{h\nu}{c} = \frac{h}{\lambda}$$

$$S = \frac{1}{2}\int d^4x\left(R + \frac{R^2}{6M^2}\right)$$

$$\Omega_m = 10$$

$$A_{ij} = \frac{8\pi h\nu^3}{c^3}B_{ij}$$

$$S_{fi} = \langle f|S|i\rangle$$

$$dY = e^{-\int_t^s V(X_{r,r})dr}\Theta(X,s)\frac{\partial u}{\partial X}\,dW$$

$$\frac{d}{dt}\langle A\rangle = \frac{1}{i\hbar}\langle[\hat{A},\hat{H}]\rangle + \left\langle\frac{\partial\hat{A}}{\partial t}\right\rangle$$

$$i\hbar\frac{\partial}{\partial t}\Psi = -\frac{\hbar^2}{2}\sum_{n=1}^{N}\frac{1}{m_n}\nabla_n^2\Psi + V\Psi$$

$$\Delta x\,\Delta p \geq \frac{\hbar}{2}$$

LEARN ABOUT
THE BIG BANG THEORY

_____
_____
_____
_____
_____
_____
_____
_____
_____
_____

LEARN ABOUT
THE BIBLICAL CREATION

_____
_____
_____
_____
_____
_____
_____
_____
_____
_____
_____

SPACE DISCOVERIES

CHOOSE A PERSON OR A TOPIC TO STUDY

(Astronauts, NASA Engineers, Astronomers, etc.)

Date:

Name:

Draw a diagram or illustration:

DESIGN YOUR OWN
SPACE FARM

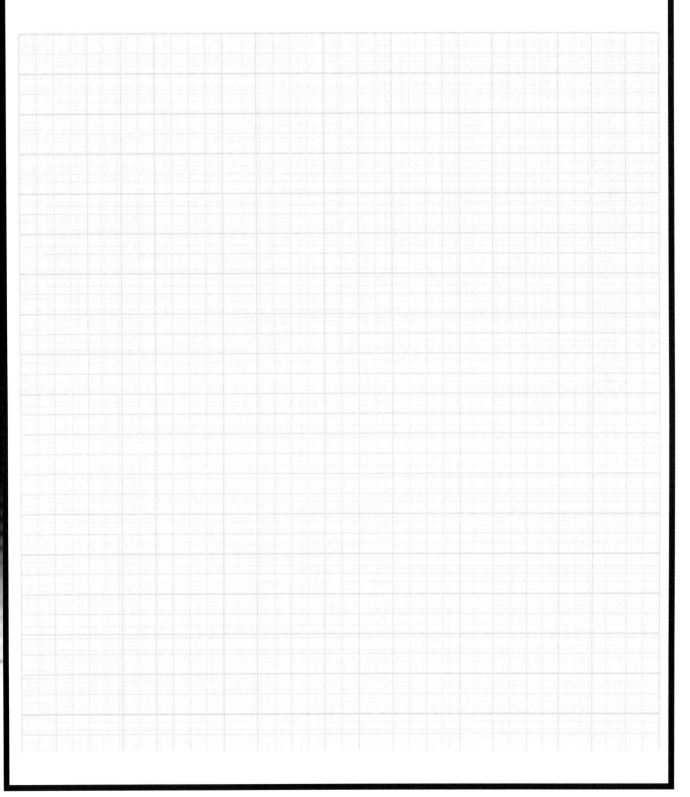

WATCH A DOCUMENTARY ABOUT SPACE

Notes:

Ideas:

Rating:
AWFUL
BAD
LAME
YUCKY
OKAY
NICE
GOOD
GREAT
SUPER
AMAZING

Title:

Topic:

Use this space to doodle

INTERESTING FACTS ABOUT THIS DOCUMENTARY:

_____
_____
_____
_____
_____

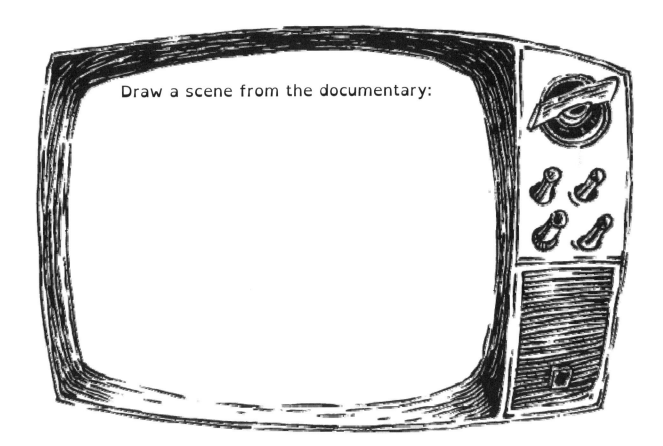

Draw a scene from the documentary:

Write a review:

_____
_____
_____
_____
_____

COLOR AND FINISH THIS PICTURE

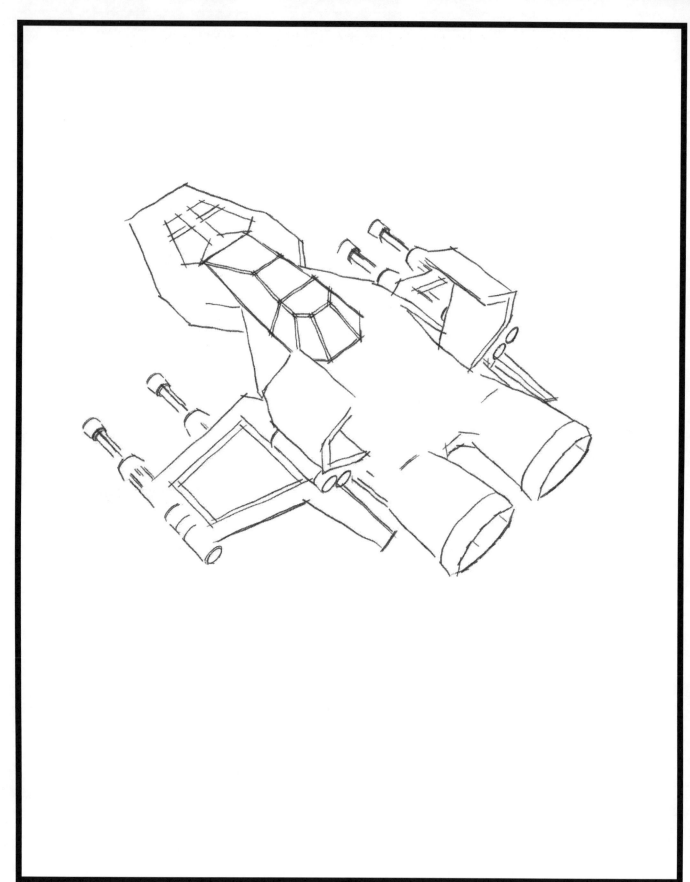

LEARN ABOUT
GRAVITATIONAL WAVES

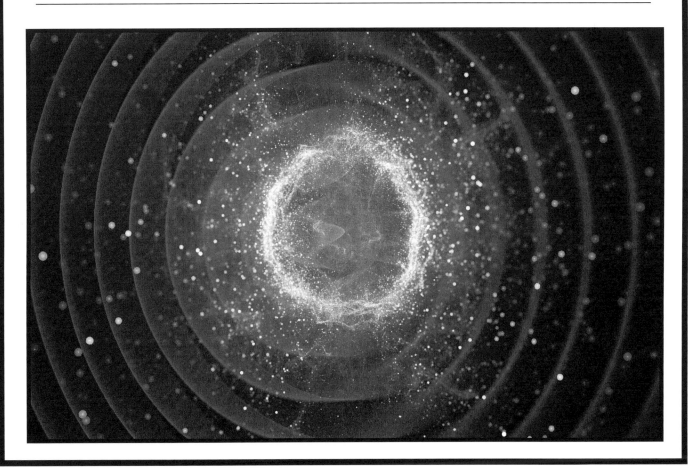

NEWS FROM SPACE

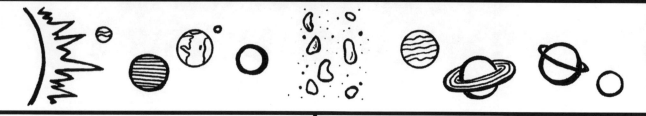

WHAT WOULD YOU LIKE TO LEARN ABOUT SPACE?

_____
_____
_____
_____
_____
_____
_____
_____

DRAW THE CURRENT PHASE OF THE MOON

SPACE IN THE NEWS
FIND PAST OR CURRENT NEWS ARTICLES AND STORIES, AND WRITE OR DRAW ABOUT THEM IN THIS SECTION

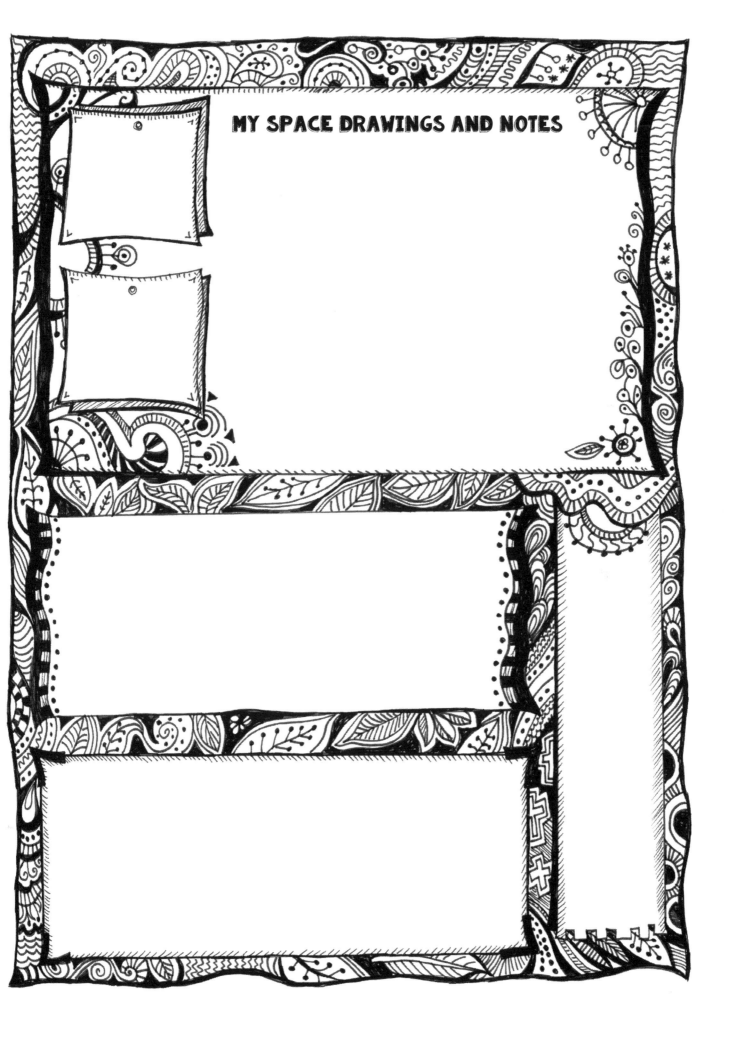

MY SPACE DRAWINGS AND NOTES

LEARN ABOUT
MINING IN SPACE

_____

_____

_____

_____

_____

_____

_____

_____

_____

_____

_____

COLOR AND FINISH THIS PICTURE

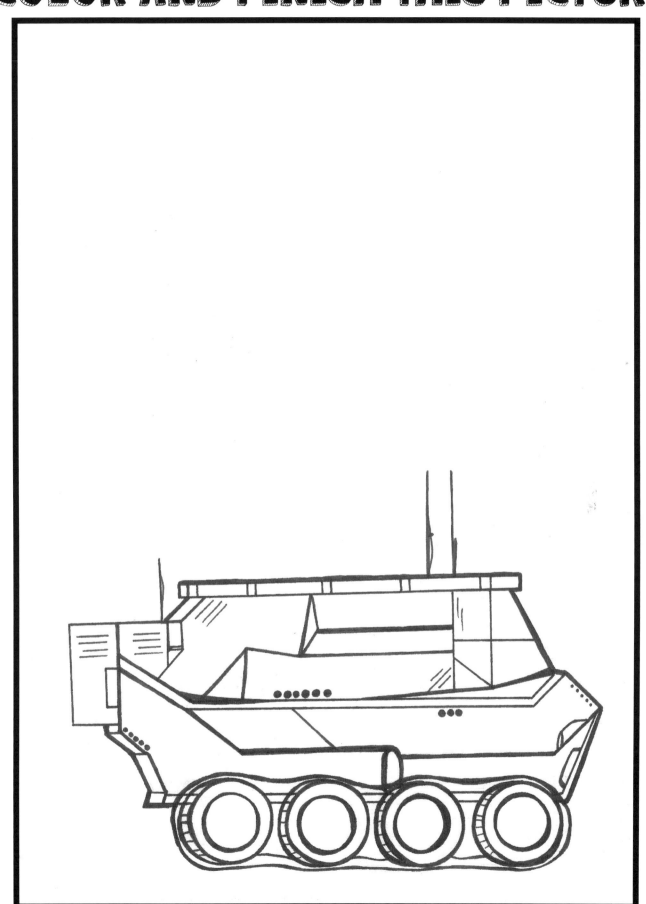

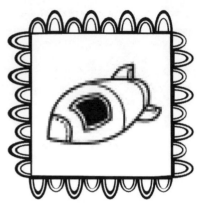

READING TIME

Today's Date:

_____

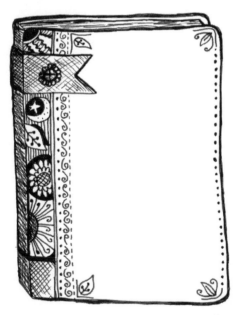

**SET YOUR TIMER FOR 30 MINUTES!
READ UNTIL THE TIMER STOPS!**

Date:

READING TIME

Copy an interesting paragraph
or list from your book.

Book Title:_____ **Page #**_____

_____
_____
_____
_____
_____
_____
_____
_____
_____
_____
_____
_____
_____

Illustration

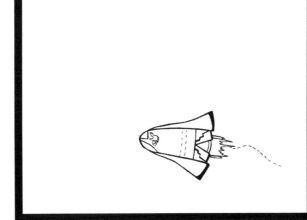

NEWS FROM SPACE

WHAT WOULD YOU LIKE TO LEARN ABOUT SPACE?

_____

_____

_____

_____

_____

_____

_____

DRAW THE CURRENT PHASE OF THE MOON

SPACE IN THE NEWS
FIND PAST OR CURRENT NEWS ARTICLES AND STORIES, AND WRITE OR DRAW ABOUT THEM IN THIS SECTION

LEARN ABOUT
INTERSTELLAR TRAVEL

What is it?
How can we travel using this method?

_____
_____
_____
_____
_____
_____
_____
_____
_____
_____
_____
_____
_____
_____
_____
_____

WATCH A DOCUMENTARY ABOUT SPACE

Notes:

Ideas:

Rating:
AWFUL
BAD
LAME
YUCKY
OKAY
NICE
GOOD
GREAT
SUPER
AMAZING

Title:

Topic:

Use this space to doodle

INTERESTING FACTS ABOUT THIS DOCUMENTARY:

_____
_____
_____
_____
_____
_____

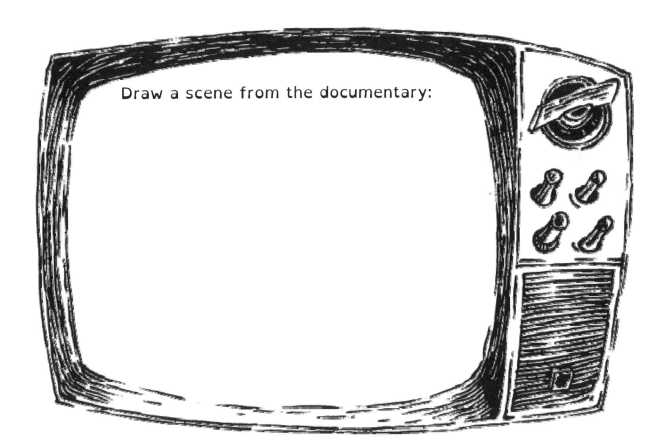

Draw a scene from the documentary:

Write a review:

_____
_____
_____
_____
_____

INTERESTING FACTS ABOUT THIS DOCUMENTARY:

SPACE DISCOVERIES

Date:

CHOOSE A PERSON OR A TOPIC TO STUDY

(Astronauts, NASA Engineers, Astronomers, etc.)

Name:_____

_____

_____

_____

_____

_____

_____

_____

_____

_____

_____

_____

_____

Draw a diagram or illustration:

MY SPACE DRAWINGS AND NOTES

SELECT A SPACE MISSION TO LEARN MORE ABOUT

The name of the mission:

_____

DATE:

_____

Write about this mission.
When and where did it take place? Who was involved?
How did it end?

_____

_____

_____

_____

_____

_____

_____

_____

_____

_____

_____

_____

LEARN ABOUT
THE KUIPER BELT

What is the Kuiper Belt?

_____

_____

_____

_____

_____

_____

_____

_____

_____

_____

_____

CREATIVE WRITING

Names & Descriptions of Characters:

_____
_____
_____
_____

Title:

_____

_____
_____
_____
_____
_____
_____
_____
_____
_____
_____
_____
_____
_____

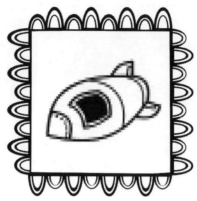

READING TIME

Today's Date:

_____

**SET YOUR TIMER FOR 30 MINUTES!
READ UNTIL THE TIMER STOPS!**

Date:

READING TIME

Copy an interesting paragraph
or list from your book.

Book Title:_____ **Page #**_____

_____

_____

_____

_____

_____

_____

_____

_____

_____

_____

_____

_____

Illustration

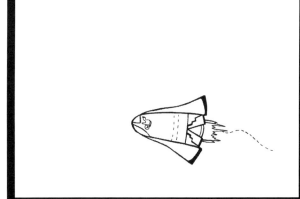

NEWS FROM SPACE

WHAT WOULD YOU LIKE TO LEARN ABOUT SPACE?

_____
_____
_____
_____
_____
_____
_____

DRAW THE CURRENT PHASE OF THE MOON

SPACE IN THE NEWS
FIND PAST OR CURRENT NEWS ARTICLES AND STORIES, AND WRITE OR DRAW ABOUT THEM IN THIS SECTION

LEARN ABOUT
SPACE TRAVEL IN THE FUTURE

_____
_____
_____
_____
_____
_____
_____
_____
_____
_____
_____
_____
_____

Draw an illustration about space travel in the future

WATCH A DOCUMENTARY ABOUT SPACE

Notes:

Ideas:

Title:

Topic:

Rating:
AWFUL
BAD
LAME
YUCKY
OKAY
NICE
GOOD
GREAT
SUPER
AMAZING

Use this space to doodle

INTERESTING FACTS ABOUT THIS DOCUMENTARY:

_____
_____
_____
_____
_____

Draw a scene from the documentary:

Write a review:

_____
_____
_____
_____
_____

Made in the USA
Monee, IL
06 July 2021